MUMBAI T|

GUIDE

2024

Your Companion Notebook to the

City of Dream

BY

JESSICA LAMPERT

Copyright © by JESSICA LAMPERT 2024. All rights reserved. Before this document is duplicated or reproduced in any manner, the publisher's consent must be gained. Therefore, the contents within can neither be stored electronically, transferred, nor kept in a database. Neither in Part nor full can the document be copied, scanned, faxed, or retained without approval from the publisher or creator

My Adventure Begins

Embarking on a journey to Mumbai, the city often referred to as the heart of India, was an experience that unfolded like a beautifully written novel, each page brimming with stories, flavors, and colors so vivid they etched themselves into my memory forever. This narrative isn't just about my journey; it's an invitation to walk with me through the bustling streets, alongside the tranquil shores, and into the soul of Mumbai, a city that never sleeps yet always dreams.

As the plane descended, the vast Arabian Sea on one side and the sprawling metropolis on the other set the stage for what was to become an unforgettable chapter in my life. Mumbai, with its pulsating energy, welcomed me with open arms. From the moment I stepped out of Chhatrapati Shivaji Maharaj International Airport, I knew I was in for a journey unlike any other.

My initial days were a whirlwind. The city's rhythm was fast, almost dizzying, yet there was a method to its madness. The blend of old-world charm with the relentless pace of modern life fascinated me. The iconic Gateway of India, standing tall against the backdrop of the sea, whispered stories of the past, while the bustling streets of Colaba Market promised adventures of their own. Each corner of this city had a story to tell, and I was eager to listen.

Navigating through Mumbai was an adventure in itself. The local trains, often referred to as the lifeline of the city, offered a glimpse into the daily life of Mumbaikars. Packed but efficient, they epitomized the spirit of Mumbai - resilient and always moving forward. The city's culinary tapestry was another revelation. From the spicy tang of street-side Vada Pav to the rich flavors of traditional Maharashtrian thalis, each meal was a journey through centuries of culinary traditions, a testament to the city's diverse cultural fabric.

Evenings in Mumbai had a different tale to tell. As the sun dipped into the Arabian Sea, the city lit up, not just with lights but with energy. Marine Drive, a crescent-shaped boulevard, became a mirror reflecting the lives of thousands who came to find solace in its view.

Here, against the sound of waves, the city's heartbeat was most palpable.

What struck me most about Mumbai was its people. Resilient, warm, and diverse, they are the true essence of the city. Their dreams and struggles, joys and sorrows, paint a vibrant mosaic of life. From the ambitious Bollywood aspirant to the hardworking street vendor, each person contributed to the city's unyielding spirit.

Mumbai is not just a destination; it's an experience, a sentiment, an ongoing festival of human spirit. Through this narrative, I invite you to see Mumbai through my eyes: a city that challenges you, changes you, and, above all, cherishes you. This journey is not just about exploring Mumbai but about discovering the myriad hues of life it offers. So, as you turn the pages of this guide, remember, Mumbai is not just a place to visit; it's a world to be experienced.

This is not just the beginning of a guide; it's the start of an adventure. Welcome to Mumbai, the city of dreams. Let's embark on this journey together, and I promise, by the end of it, you'll not just visit Mumbai, you'll live it.

Table of Content

My Adventure Begins

Chapter 1 Introduction to Mumbai

    The Heart of Mumbai: Understanding the City's Soul

    Mumbai Through the Ages: A Brief History

    Navigating the Cultural Melting Pot: Diversity and Tradition

    Mumbai Today: A Metropolis in Motion

Chapter 2 Before You Go: Essential Travel Information

    Planning Your Trip: Best Times to Visit

    Visas and Entry Requirements: What You Need to Know

    Getting There: Air, Land, and Sea Options

    Packing Tips and What to Bring

Chapter 3 Settling In: Accommodation and Local Transport

    Choosing Your Nest: From Luxury to Budget Accommodations

    Navigating the City: Public Transport Explained

　　　　Taxi, Auto-Rickshaw, and Ride-Sharing: Tips for Smooth Rides

　　　　Safety Tips and How to Avoid Common Scams

Chapter 4 Savor the Flavor: Dining and Cuisine

　　　　Street Food Galore: Must-Try Dishes

　　　　Fine Dining in Mumbai: A Culinary Journey

　　　　Vegetarian Delights: A Taste of Mumbai's Vegetarian Cuisine

　　　　Food Tours and Cooking Classes: Immersive Culinary Experiences

Chapter 5 After Dark: Exploring Mumbai's Nightlife

　　　　Clubs and Bars: Where to Enjoy Mumbai at Night

　　　　Cultural Performances and Theatre: Nighttime Arts

　　　　Night Markets and Late-Night Eats: A Different Side of Mumbai

　　　　Safety Tips for Night Owls

Chapter 6 Must-Visit Attractions in Mumbai

The Gateway of India: A Symbolic Arch
The Chhatrapati Shivaji Maharaj Terminus: Architectural Marvel
Marine Drive: Mumbai's Seaside Promenade
Elephanta Caves: A UNESCO World Heritage Site

Chapter 7 Day Trips and Excursions
Alibaug: Beach Bliss
Lonavala and Khandala: Hill Stations Near Mumbai
Matheran: A Vehicle-Free Hill Station Experience
The Kanheri Caves: Ancient Buddhist Caves

Chapter 8 Museums and Galleries
The Chhatrapati Shivaji Maharaj Vastu Sangrahalaya: Art and History
The National Gallery of Modern Art: Contemporary Insights
Dr. Bhau Daji Lad Mumbai City Museum: Mumbai's Rich Heritage

> The Jehangir Art Gallery: A Hub for Modern Art

Chapter 9 Shopping and Souvenirs
> Colaba Causeway: Shopper's Paradise
>
> Crawford Market: A Blend of Old and New
>
> Chor Bazaar: The Thieves Market
>
> Local Handicrafts and Where to Find Them

Chapter 10 Practical Tips for the Smart Traveler
> Staying Connected: SIM Cards and Wi-Fi
>
> Health and Safety: Hospitals and Emergency Contacts
>
> Cultural Etiquette: Dos and Don'ts
>
> Parting Thoughts: Leaving Mumbai with Memories

Conclusion

Chapter 1

Introduction to Mumbai

The Heart of Mumbai: Understanding the City's Soul

To understand the soul of Mumbai, one must journey through its vibrant history, from its early inhabitants to its present status as the bustling metropolis known as the financial, commercial, and entertainment capital of India. This exploration is not just about tracing the city's physical growth but about delving into the essence that makes Mumbai, formerly known as Bombay, a city unlike any other.

From Fishing Villages to a Colonial Centerpiece

Mumbai's story begins where the sea meets the land; the city's earliest residents were the Koli people, a community of fishermen whose rhythms of life were dictated by the tides. The seven islands that constituted Mumbai were lush with greenery and teeming with life, a stark contrast to the city's current skyline dominated by skyscrapers and bustling streets.

In the 16th century, the Portuguese colonizers took control, renaming it Bom Bahia, or "The Good Bay." However, it was under the British East India Company that Mumbai truly began its transformation. The British saw Mumbai's potential as a strategic trading port, leading to the reclamation project that unified the seven islands into a singular landmass. This era marked the beginning of Mumbai's metamorphosis.

The Birth of the Modern Metropolis

The construction of the Suez Canal in 1869 was a pivotal moment, positioning Mumbai as a major shipping hub on the international trade route. The city's landscape began to change, with Gothic and Victorian architecture marking its status as the "Urbs Prima in Indis" or the "First City of India." The cotton mills flourished, attracting a wave of migrants and transforming the city into a melting pot of cultures, religions, and languages.

The 20th century saw Mumbai becoming a hotbed for the independence movement against British rule. The city was at the forefront, with figures like Bal Gangadhar Tilak and Mahatma Gandhi leading the charge from its streets. The Quit India Movement's call was made in Mumbai in 1942, a decisive moment in India's struggle for freedom.

Mumbai Today: A City of Dreams

In the post-independence era, Mumbai continued to grow exponentially, both in population and in stature. The establishment of the Bollywood film industry added a new dimension to its cultural landscape, making it the epicenter of Indian cinema. The city's financial institutions, such as the Bombay Stock Exchange, reinforced its position as the economic powerhouse of India.

Yet, the heart of Mumbai beats strongest in its diversity and resilience. The city is a juxtaposition of the ultra-rich and the struggling poor, of gleaming high-rises and sprawling slums, of tranquil sea faces and chaotic local trains. It's in these contrasts that Mumbai's soul lies, a testament to its history of welcoming and integrating a myriad of people, dreams, and aspirations.

The Unbreakable Spirit

The resilience of Mumbai has been tested time and again, be it through natural disasters or terrorist attacks. The floods of 2005, the terrorist attacks of 2008, and numerous other crises have seen the city bending but never breaking. The unity and strength of Mumbaikars in the face of adversity embody the indomitable spirit of the city.

Understanding the heart of Mumbai is to recognize its ability to embrace change while holding onto the threads of history, culture, and diversity that weave together its unique identity. It's a city that doesn't just survive; it thrives, pulsating with life and energy, inviting all to be a part of its ongoing story.

Mumbai's soul is mirrored in the Arabian Sea it overlooks—vast, mysterious, and enduring. It's a city that captures the heart of every visitor, leaving an indelible mark with its vibrant streets, its enduring landmarks, and, most importantly, its people. To know Mumbai is to understand the resilience, diversity, and vibrancy that define not just a city, but a way of life.

Mumbai Through the Ages: A Brief History

Mumbai, a city woven from the threads of myriad histories, cultures, and aspirations, offers a compelling narrative that spans centuries. Its journey from a cluster of seven marshy islands to the bustling, vibrant metropolis we know today is a testament to human ambition, resilience, and the ceaseless march of time. To explore Mumbai's history is to uncover the layers that form the bedrock of this city's indomitable spirit.

The Early Inhabitants and Colonial Encounters

The story of Mumbai begins with its earliest known residents, the Koli fishermen, adept in navigating the Arabian Sea's waters, relying on fishing and salt panning for their livelihood. These islands were part of a kingdom ruled by various indigenous dynasties before the arrival of Islamic rulers in the 14th century. The strategic importance of the islands was recognized early on due to their location along the maritime route.

The arrival of the Portuguese in the 16th century marked the first significant shift in control, with the islands being ceded to Portugal by the Sultan of Gujarat in 1534. Renamed Bom Bahia, or "Good

Bay," the Portuguese established their stronghold, introducing their culture, religion, and architectural style to the landscape.

The British Era and the Unification of the Islands

The true transformation of Mumbai began in the mid-17th century when the islands were handed over to the British East India Company as part of the dowry in the marriage of Portugal's Princess Catherine of Braganza to England's Charles II. The British saw the potential of the deep natural harbor and set about connecting the disparate islands into a cohesive landmass, a project that would take over 150 years to complete.

Under British rule, Mumbai rapidly transformed into a major trade and industrial center. The construction of the Suez Canal further elevated its importance, making it a crucial stopover on the maritime route to the East. The cotton mills of Mumbai became the backbone of its economy, attracting labor from across India and turning the city into a melting pot of cultures, languages, and religions.

The Independence Movement and Post-Colonial Growth

The 20th century was a turbulent yet transformative period for Mumbai. The city played a pivotal role in India's struggle for independence, hosting significant events and movements that challenged British colonial rule. Post-independence, Mumbai continued to flourish, evolving into a global financial hub and the birthplace of Bollywood, which would go on to become one of the largest centers of film production in the world.

The latter half of the 20th century and the early 21st century saw Mumbai expanding its economic, cultural, and social horizons. The city's skyline began to soar, and its population burgeoned, making it one of the most populous cities globally.

Resilience in the Face of Adversity

Mumbai's history is also marked by its resilience in the face of challenges. Natural disasters, terrorist attacks, and social unrest have tested the city's spirit. Yet, time and again, Mumbai has emerged stronger, with its people displaying unparalleled solidarity and strength.

A City That Dreams

Today, Mumbai stands as a testament to human endeavor, a city that dreams big and achieves bigger. It is not just the economic heart of India but also a cultural cauldron where traditions and modernity blend seamlessly. Mumbai's history is a mirror to its soul—a resilient, vibrant, and dynamic force that propels it forward.

Navigating the Cultural Melting Pot: Diversity and Tradition

Mumbai, often referred to as the 'Maximum City', is as much a crucible of diverse cultures as it is a beacon of enduring traditions. Its fabric is woven from the threads of myriad communities, languages, festivals, and culinary traditions, making it a microcosm of India itself. Navigating through Mumbai's cultural landscape is akin to traversing the breadth of the country, offering insights into the unity and diversity that define India.

A Tapestry of Communities

The cultural diversity of Mumbai is its most defining characteristic. Home to indigenous communities like the Kolis, the original inhabitants and fishermen of the region, Mumbai has, over centuries, welcomed waves of migrants. These include Gujaratis, Marathis, Konkanis, Parsis, Sindhis, and a significant population of North Indians, South Indians, and a host of other communities from across the country.

Each group has contributed to the city's social fabric, bringing in their unique customs, festivals, languages, and culinary flavors.

The Festival Kaleidoscope

Mumbai's calendar is dotted with festivals celebrated with great fervor, showcasing the city's pluralistic ethos. Ganesh Chaturthi stands out as a spectacular public event, uniting the city in a ten-day gala of devotion, music, and dance in honor of Lord Ganesha. Eid, Diwali, Christmas, Navratri, and the Parsi New Year are celebrated with equal enthusiasm, reflecting the city's secular spirit. The Kala Ghoda Arts Festival and the Mumbai Film Festival highlight its status as a cultural hub, drawing artists, filmmakers, and enthusiasts from around the globe.

Culinary Confluence

The culinary landscape of Mumbai is as diverse as its population. Street food, like Vada Pav, Pav Bhaji, and Bhel Puri, offers a taste of the city's bustling life, while traditional Maharashtrian cuisine showcases the region's flavors. The influence of the Konkani, Goan, Gujarati, Parsi, and Sindhi communities is evident in the city's varied dining scene. Mumbai's coastal location means seafood is a staple for many, prepared in styles unique to the different communities residing here.

Language and Literature

Marathi is the state language and carries a rich literary heritage, but Mumbai's linguistic landscape is incredibly varied. Hindi, English, Gujarati, Urdu, and Konkani are among the many languages spoken, contributing to the city's vibrant literary and cultural scene. Mumbai has a robust tradition of theatre in multiple languages, including Marathi, Gujarati, and Hindi, reflecting the city's diverse cultural tapestry.

Architecture: A Historical Palimpsest

Mumbai's architecture narrates the city's history, from the ancient Elephanta Caves to the Victorian Gothic and Art Deco buildings of the British era, and the modern skyscrapers that symbolize its economic aspirations. The city's landscape is a testament to its evolving identity, accommodating the old with the new in a seamless narrative.

Tradition and Modernity: A Delicate Balance

In the midst of rapid urbanization and globalization, Mumbai manages to preserve its cultural heritage while embracing modernity. Traditional art forms, festivals, and culinary practices coexist with contemporary art, music, and lifestyle, making Mumbai a city that is rooted yet forward-looking.

Navigating Mumbai's cultural melting pot is an enriching journey through the heart of India's diversity and tradition. It offers a glimpse into the coexistence of multiple identities within a shared geographical space, united by a common spirit of resilience, aspiration, and communal harmony. Mumbai stands not just as a city but as a testament to the enduring power of diversity and tradition in shaping human societies.

Mumbai Today: A Metropolis in Motion

Mumbai, a city perpetually in motion, mirrors the dynamism and resilience of its people and the dreams that fuel their daily endeavors. Today, it stands as a sprawling metropolis, an amalgamation of aspirations, cultures, and relentless energy, navigating the complexities of modern urban life while striving towards a future marked by innovation and growth. This city, pulsating with life, offers a unique snapshot of a society in constant flux, embodying the challenges and triumphs of urban India in the 21st century.

Economic Powerhouse

At the heart of Mumbai's ceaseless activity is its status as India's financial capital. Home to the Bombay Stock Exchange, Reserve Bank of India, and numerous multinational corporations, the city is the epicenter of the country's economic life. It generates a significant portion of India's GDP, with key industries including finance, gems and jewelry, leather processing, IT, and entertainment, particularly Bollywood—the heartthrob of the nation and a global cinematic phenomenon.

Cultural Vibrancy

Mumbai's cultural landscape is as diverse as its population. The city is a melting pot of traditions, languages, and artistic expressions, hosting vibrant festivals, theater productions, music concerts, and art exhibitions that reflect its multicultural ethos. The annual Mumbai Film Festival and the Kala Ghoda Arts Festival are just two highlights of the city's rich cultural calendar, drawing talent and audiences from across the world.

Architectural Marvels and Green Spaces

The architecture of Mumbai is a testament to its historical layers and cosmopolitan present. From the iconic Gateway of India, a symbol of the colonial past, to the contemporary skyline defined by skyscrapers and luxury complexes, the city's built environment is a study in contrasts. Amidst the urban sprawl, green spaces like the Sanjay Gandhi National Park, the largest urban park located within a city limit worldwide, and the seaside promenades at Marine Drive and Bandstand offer residents and visitors a respite from the hustle and bustle.

Challenges of Urbanization

Mumbai's rapid growth has not been without its challenges. The city grapples with issues typical of urban expansion, including housing shortages, traffic congestion, pollution, and social inequality. The contrast between affluent neighborhoods and sprawling slums highlights the economic disparities that define urban existence. Yet, efforts to address these challenges through infrastructure development, slum rehabilitation projects, and environmental initiatives reflect Mumbai's commitment to sustainable and inclusive growth.

A City of Innovation and Aspiration

Innovation thrives in the hustle of Mumbai, with startups and tech companies burgeoning, driven by a young, ambitious population keen on solving urban and social challenges. Educational institutions and research centers in and around Mumbai contribute to its status as a hub of learning and innovation.

Resilience and Spirit

Perhaps Mumbai's most defining characteristic is the resilience and spirit of its residents. Known as Mumbaikars, the people of Mumbai are celebrated for their ability to persevere through challenges, be it natural disasters, terrorist attacks, or the everyday struggles of urban life. This indomitable spirit is what binds the city together, driving it forward with hope and determination.

Chapter 2

Before You Go: Essential Travel Information

Planning Your Trip: Best Times to Visit

Choosing the right time to visit Mumbai can greatly enhance your experience and enjoyment of the city. Mumbai experiences a tropical climate with distinct seasons, each offering unique attractions and challenges for travelers. Understanding the weather patterns, cultural events, and tourist crowds can help you plan your trip effectively.

Weather Overview

Mumbai's weather is influenced by its coastal location, resulting in hot and humid conditions throughout the year. The city experiences three primary seasons:

Summer (March to June): Summers in Mumbai are hot and humid, with temperatures often soaring above 30°C (86°F). The months of April and May are typically the hottest, with temperatures occasionally touching 40°C (104°F). Humidity levels can be quite high, making outdoor activities uncomfortable for some visitors.

Monsoon (June to September): The monsoon season brings heavy rainfall to Mumbai, providing relief from the scorching summer heat. Monsoon showers usually arrive in June and continue through September, with July and August receiving the highest rainfall. The city comes alive with lush greenery during this time, but flooding and waterlogging are common, leading to traffic disruptions.

Winter (October to February): Winter is the most pleasant time to visit Mumbai, with cooler temperatures and lower humidity levels. Daytime temperatures range from 20°C to 30°C (68°F to 86°F), while nights can be slightly cooler. This season is ideal for exploring outdoor attractions and enjoying cultural events without the discomfort of excessive heat.

Best Times to Visit

November to February: Winter is considered the best time to visit Mumbai, as the weather is pleasant, and outdoor activities are enjoyable. This period coincides with several festivals and cultural events, including Diwali, Christmas, and the Kala Ghoda Arts Festival in February, offering visitors a chance to immerse themselves in the city's vibrant culture.

March to May: While summers can be hot and humid, this period also sees fewer tourists, making it a good time to explore Mumbai's attractions without the crowds. If you can tolerate the heat, you may find better deals on accommodations and flights during this offseason.

Late June to September: While the monsoon season can be challenging due to heavy rainfall and waterlogging, it also offers a unique experience for adventurous travelers. Witnessing

Mumbai come alive in the rains, enjoying hot snacks and chai by the sea, and experiencing the city's resilience during monsoon showers can be memorable experiences.

Considerations for Peak Seasons

During peak tourist seasons, especially in winter, it's advisable to book accommodations and transportation in advance to avoid last-minute hassles. Popular attractions may also experience longer queues and crowded conditions, so planning your itinerary wisely can help you make the most of your time in Mumbai.

Ultimately, the best time to visit Mumbai depends on your preferences, tolerance for heat and humidity, and the experiences you seek. Whether you choose to embrace the energy of summer, the lushness of monsoon, or the pleasantness of winter, Mumbai welcomes you with open arms, ready to enchant you with its myriad charms and experiences.

Visas and Entry Requirements: What You Need to Know

For travelers planning a visit to Mumbai, understanding the visa and entry requirements is essential to ensure a smooth and hassle-free journey. Navigating the visa application process, understanding the types of visas available, and complying with entry regulations are crucial steps in planning your trip to Mumbai.

Visa Requirements

Tourist Visa: Most visitors to India, including Mumbai, require a tourist visa. Tourist visas are typically valid for multiple entries within a specified period, usually ranging from 30 days to 10 years, depending on the nationality of the traveler and the type of visa applied for.

e-Visa: India offers an e-Visa facility for citizens of eligible countries, allowing them to apply for a tourist visa online. The e-Visa is available for short stays of up to 60 days, with options for single-entry, double-entry, or multiple-entry visas. Travelers must apply for the e-Visa at least four days before their intended date of travel.

Visa on Arrival: Some nationalities may be eligible for a visa on arrival, which allows travelers to obtain a tourist visa upon arrival at select airports in India, including Mumbai's Chhatrapati Shivaji Maharaj International Airport. However, it's essential to check eligibility criteria and requirements before opting for this option.

Documents Required

When applying for a tourist visa or e-Visa to Mumbai, travelers typically need to provide the following documents:

- Passport with a minimum validity of six months from the date of arrival in India.
- Completed visa application form with accurate information.

- Recent passport-sized photographs as per specifications.
- Proof of travel arrangements, such as flight tickets or itinerary.
- Proof of accommodation arrangements, such as hotel reservations or a letter of invitation from a host in India.
- Proof of sufficient funds to cover expenses during the stay in India.

Application Process

Online Application: For e-Visa applications, travelers need to fill out the online application form on the official website of the Indian government's e-Visa portal. The form requires personal details, passport information, travel plans, and other relevant information.

Submission and Payment: After completing the application form, travelers need to upload supporting documents and make the visa fee payment online. The fee varies depending on the type of visa and nationality of the applicant.

Approval and Issuance: Once the application is submitted and payment is made, the visa processing time is usually within a few business days. Approved e-Visas are sent to the applicant's email address, and travelers are required to carry a printout of the e-Visa approval for verification upon arrival in India.

Entry Regulations

Upon arrival in Mumbai, travelers must present their valid passport, visa (e-Visa printout or visa stamp), and completed arrival form to immigration authorities for verification.

Immigration officers may conduct interviews or request additional documents, so travelers should be prepared to provide information about their stay, purpose of visit, and onward travel plans.

Visitors are generally granted a stay of up to the validity period of their visa, but it's essential to adhere to the authorized duration of stay to avoid overstaying and potential penalties.

Understanding the visa and entry requirements for Mumbai is crucial for a hassle-free travel experience. By familiarizing yourself with the application process, required documents, and entry regulations, you can ensure a smooth journey and focus on enjoying all that Mumbai has to offer, from its vibrant culture to its bustling streets and iconic landmarks.

Getting There: Air, Land, and Sea Options

Mumbai, being one of India's major metropolitan cities and a significant international hub, offers various transportation options for travelers arriving from different parts of the world. Whether you're flying in from abroad, arriving from within India, or exploring sea routes, understanding the available modes of transportation can help you plan your journey to Mumbai efficiently.

Air Travel

Chhatrapati Shivaji Maharaj International Airport (BOM): Mumbai's primary gateway is the Chhatrapati Shivaji Maharaj International Airport, located in the suburb of Andheri. It serves as a major hub for both domestic and international flights, connecting Mumbai to cities across India and around the world.

International Flights: Several airlines operate direct international flights to Mumbai from major cities worldwide, including London, Dubai, Singapore, New York, and Hong Kong, among others. Indirect flights with layovers are also available from a broader range of destinations.

Domestic Flights: Mumbai is well-connected to domestic destinations across India, with frequent flights operated by airlines such as IndiGo, Air India, SpiceJet, and Vistara. Domestic flights to Mumbai operate from major cities like Delhi, Bangalore, Kolkata, Chennai, and Hyderabad, among others.

Land Travel

Railways: Mumbai is a major railway hub, with several railway stations serving different parts of the city. The two primary railway terminals are Chhatrapati Shivaji Maharaj Terminus (CST) and Mumbai Central. Mumbai is connected to various cities across India via a vast network of Indian Railways trains, including long-distance express trains and suburban commuter trains.

Roadways: Mumbai is well-connected to neighboring cities and states via a network of national highways and expressways. State-run buses, private coaches, and taxis ply between Mumbai and nearby destinations, providing convenient road travel options for visitors.

Sea Travel

Cruise Terminal: Mumbai has a dedicated cruise terminal, the Mumbai Port Trust's International Cruise Terminal, located at Ballard Pier. The terminal serves as a point of embarkation and disembarkation for cruise ships operating in the Arabian Sea. Several cruise lines offer itineraries that include Mumbai as a port of call, connecting the city to destinations across Asia and beyond.

Transportation within Mumbai

Once you've arrived in Mumbai, various modes of transportation are available for getting around the city:

Local Trains: Mumbai's suburban railway network, known as the "lifeline" of the city, provides an efficient and economical means of commuting within Mumbai and its suburbs.

Metro: Mumbai Metro operates several lines connecting different parts of the city, providing a fast and convenient mode of transport, particularly for longer distances.

Taxis and Auto-rickshaws: Metered taxis and auto-rickshaws are readily available for short-distance travel within the city. Ride-hailing services like Uber and Ola are also popular options.

Buses: Brihanmumbai Electric Supply and Transport (BEST) operates a vast fleet of buses covering various routes within Mumbai, offering an affordable mode of transportation for travelers.

With its well-developed transportation infrastructure, Mumbai offers multiple options for travelers to reach the city conveniently and explore its diverse attractions. Whether you prefer air, land, or sea travel, Mumbai welcomes you with open arms, ready to embark on an unforgettable journey through its vibrant streets, cultural landmarks, and dynamic neighborhoods.

Packing Tips and What to Bring

Packing for a trip to Mumbai requires careful consideration of the city's climate, culture, and activities you plan to engage in during your stay. From lightweight clothing to essential accessories, here are some packing tips and items to bring along to ensure a comfortable and enjoyable experience in Mumbai.

Clothing

Lightweight and Breathable Clothes: Mumbai has a tropical climate with hot and humid weather for most of the year. Pack lightweight, breathable clothing made from natural fabrics like cotton and linen to stay cool and comfortable.

Modest Clothing: While Mumbai is cosmopolitan and generally accepting of diverse clothing styles, it's advisable to dress modestly, especially when visiting religious sites or traditional neighborhoods. Consider packing modest tops, pants, and knee-length skirts or dresses.

Comfortable Footwear: Opt for comfortable and sturdy footwear suitable for walking, as you'll likely be exploring Mumbai's bustling streets and landmarks. Sandals, sneakers, or walking shoes are ideal choices.

Rain Gear: If you're visiting Mumbai during the monsoon season (June to September), pack a lightweight rain jacket or poncho, as well as waterproof footwear, to stay dry during sudden downpours.

Accessories

Sun Protection: Mumbai's sun can be intense, especially during the summer months. Bring sunglasses, a wide-brimmed hat or cap, and sunscreen with a high SPF to protect your skin from harmful UV rays.

Reusable Water Bottle: Stay hydrated by carrying a refillable water bottle with you. Mumbai's tap water is not potable, so opt for bottled water or use a portable water purifier to refill your bottle from filtered sources.

Daypack or Backpack: A lightweight daypack or backpack is essential for carrying essentials like water, snacks, sunscreen, and a camera while exploring Mumbai's attractions.

Travel Adapter and Converter: Mumbai uses the Type D electrical socket, so be sure to pack a suitable travel adapter if your devices have a different plug type. Additionally, a voltage converter may be necessary for appliances that are not dual voltage.

Personal Essentials

Travel Documents: Carry essential travel documents, including your passport, visa (if applicable), flight tickets, hotel reservations, and any other relevant identification or permits.

Medications and First Aid Kit: Pack any prescription medications, over-the-counter remedies, and a basic first aid kit containing bandages, antiseptic wipes, pain relievers, and any other personal medications or supplies you may need.

Personal Hygiene Items: Bring toiletries such as toothpaste, toothbrush, shampoo, conditioner, soap, and any other personal hygiene items you require. While these items are readily available in Mumbai, you may prefer to use your preferred brands.

Travel Insurance: Consider purchasing travel insurance to cover unforeseen circumstances such as medical emergencies, trip cancellations, or lost luggage during your visit to Mumbai.

Cultural Considerations

Modest Attire for Religious Sites: If you plan to visit temples, mosques, or other religious sites, pack clothing that covers your shoulders, arms, and knees as a sign of respect.

Comfortable Sleepwear: Mumbai's climate can be warm and humid, so pack lightweight and breathable sleepwear for a comfortable night's rest.

By packing wisely and considering Mumbai's climate, culture, and activities, you can ensure a comfortable and enjoyable trip to this vibrant city. Remember to leave space in your luggage for souvenirs and mementos to cherish the memories of your time in Mumbai.

Chapter 3

Settling In: Accommodation and Local Transport

Choosing Your Nest: From Luxury to Budget Accommodations

When it comes to finding the perfect place to stay in Mumbai, travelers are spoiled for choice, with options ranging from luxurious hotels to budget-friendly accommodations. Whether you seek opulent amenities or value for money, Mumbai offers a diverse array of lodging options to suit every preference and budget.

- **Luxury Hotels**

Taj Mahal Palace, Mumbai

Location: Apollo Bandar, Colaba, Mumbai.

Overview: Situated overlooking the Arabian Sea, Taj Mahal Palace is an iconic landmark renowned for its grandeur, impeccable service, and timeless elegance. Boasting opulent rooms and suites adorned with lavish furnishings, the hotel offers a range of dining options, a spa, swimming pool, and unparalleled views of the Gateway of India.

Cost: Starting from ₹15,000 per night.

The Oberoi, Mumbai

Location: Nariman Point, Mumbai.

Overview: Nestled in the heart of Mumbai's business district, The Oberoi epitomizes luxury and sophistication. With meticulously appointed rooms, exquisite dining venues, a rooftop pool, and a spa offering rejuvenating treatments, this hotel provides an oasis of tranquility amidst the bustling cityscape.

Cost: Starting from ₹18,000 per night.

- **Boutique Hotels**

Abode Bombay

Location: Colaba, Mumbai.

Overview: Abode Bombay offers a charming blend of heritage and contemporary design, with individually styled rooms reflecting the city's eclectic spirit. Located in the vibrant Colaba neighborhood, the hotel provides personalized service, a cozy communal lounge, and easy access to iconic landmarks such as the Gateway of India and Colaba Causeway.

Cost: Starting from ₹7,000 per night.

Svenska Design Hotel

Location: Andheri West, Mumbai.

Overview: Combining chic aesthetics with modern comforts, Svenska Design Hotel is a stylish retreat in Mumbai's bustling Andheri West district. Featuring sleek rooms, an alfresco poolside lounge, a gourmet restaurant, and a fully equipped fitness center, the hotel offers a contemporary urban escape for discerning travelers.

Cost: Starting from ₹5,000 per night.

- **Budget Accommodations**

Backpacker Panda Colaba

Location: Colaba, Mumbai.

Overview: Catering to budget-conscious travelers, Backpacker Panda Colaba offers clean and cozy dormitory rooms and private suites in a prime location near Colaba Causeway and Mumbai's major attractions. With a vibrant backpacker atmosphere, communal kitchen facilities, and organized city tours, it provides an affordable and sociable stay experience.

Cost: Starting from ₹700 per night (dormitory).

Hotel Sea Lord

Location: Colaba, Mumbai.

Overview: Located in the heart of South Mumbai, Hotel Sea Lord offers simple yet comfortable accommodations at budget-friendly rates. With clean rooms, attentive service, and proximity to popular landmarks like the Gateway of India and Marine Drive, it provides excellent value for money for travelers exploring the city on a budget.

Cost: Starting from ₹2,000 per night.

Whether you're indulging in luxury, seeking boutique charm, or prioritizing affordability, Mumbai's diverse accommodation options ensure a memorable stay tailored to your preferences and budget. From iconic five-star hotels to cozy backpacker hostels, each establishment offers its own unique blend of comfort, convenience, and hospitality amidst the bustling cityscape of Mumbai.

Navigating the City: Public Transport Explained

Mumbai's bustling streets and vibrant neighborhoods are best explored using its extensive public transportation network, which includes trains, buses, metro, taxis, auto-rickshaws, and ferries. Understanding how to navigate these options can help you efficiently traverse the city and experience its diverse attractions.

Mumbai Local Trains

Overview: Mumbai's local trains, operated by Indian Railways, are the lifeline of the city, connecting its suburbs and beyond. Divided into Western Line, Central Line, and Harbour Line, these trains provide a rapid and cost-effective means of commuting for millions of residents daily.

Cost: Fares are distance-based and extremely affordable, with tickets ranging from ₹10 to ₹50 for a single journey, depending on the distance traveled.

Accessibility: Local trains can be crowded during peak hours, so be prepared for a bustling commute. Ladies' compartments are available for female passengers.

Mumbai Metro

Overview: Mumbai Metro is a relatively newer addition to the city's public transportation system, offering a faster and more comfortable alternative for commuters. Currently, there are two operational metro lines: Line 1

(Versova-Andheri-Ghatkopar) and Line 7 (Dahisar-Andheri East).

Cost: Metro fares are distance-based, starting from ₹10 for short trips and going up to ₹50 or more for longer journeys.

Accessibility: Metro trains are air-conditioned and less crowded compared to local trains, making them a preferred option for tourists and commuters alike.

BEST Buses

Overview: Brihanmumbai Electric Supply and Transport (BEST) operates a vast fleet of buses that ply across Mumbai and its suburbs, providing extensive coverage of the city. Buses are available in various categories, including ordinary, express, and AC buses.

Cost: Bus fares are distance-based, with tickets starting from ₹5 for short distances and going up to ₹25 or more for longer routes.

Accessibility: Buses are a budget-friendly option for getting around Mumbai, but they can be affected by traffic congestion during peak hours.

Taxis and Auto-rickshaws

Overview: Taxis and auto-rickshaws are popular modes of transportation for short-distance travel within the city. Taxis operate on metered fares, while auto-rickshaw fares are negotiated or based on pre-set tariffs.

Cost: Taxi fares start from ₹25 for the first kilometer and approximately ₹15 per kilometer thereafter. Auto-rickshaw fares start from ₹18 for the first kilometer and approximately ₹12 per kilometer thereafter.

Accessibility: Taxis and auto-rickshaws are readily available throughout the city, but be sure to negotiate fares or ensure meters are used to avoid overcharging.

Ferries

Overview: Mumbai's coastal location allows for ferry services that connect different parts of the city, including popular destinations like Elephanta Island and Alibaug. These ferries offer scenic views of the Arabian Sea and provide an alternative mode of transportation for travelers.

Cost: Ferry fares vary depending on the route and distance traveled, ranging from ₹50 to ₹300 or more for a one-way trip.

Accessibility: Ferries are a unique way to explore Mumbai's coastal areas and nearby islands, offering a refreshing break from the city's hustle and bustle.

By leveraging Mumbai's diverse public transportation options, travelers can navigate the city's bustling streets, vibrant markets, and iconic landmarks with ease. Whether you're commuting to work, exploring tourist attractions, or simply soaking in the sights and sounds of Mumbai, the city's efficient and extensive public transport system ensures a convenient and memorable experience for all.

Taxi, Auto-Rickshaw, and Ride-Sharing: Tips for Smooth Rides

Navigating Mumbai's bustling streets can be an adventure in itself, especially when it comes to choosing the right mode of transportation. Whether you're opting for a traditional taxi, an auto-rickshaw, or a modern ride-sharing service, here are some tips to ensure your journey is smooth and hassle-free:

- **Choose Reputable Services**

Taxi:

Opt for licensed taxi services such as Meru, Mega Cabs, or TabCab. These companies typically maintain their vehicles well and adhere to standard fare rates.

Auto-Rickshaw:

Look for auto-rickshaws with meters, and ensure the driver agrees to use it before starting your journey. Refrain from boarding autos without meters, as they may overcharge you.

Ride-Sharing:

Stick to well-known ride-sharing apps like Uber or Ola. These apps provide transparent pricing and driver ratings, ensuring a safer and more reliable experience.

- **Confirm Fare Rates**

Taxi:

Before boarding a taxi, confirm that the driver agrees to use the meter. If the meter is not functional, negotiate the fare upfront to avoid disputes later.

Auto-Rickshaw:

Check the auto-rickshaw fare chart displayed on the vehicle or request an estimate from the driver before starting your journey. Ensure there are no hidden charges.

Ride-Sharing:

Verify the fare estimate on the ride-sharing app before confirming your booking. This helps prevent unexpected surcharges or price discrepancies.

- **Know Your Route**

Taxi:

If you're familiar with the route, guide the driver accordingly. Otherwise, use navigation apps like Google Maps to ensure you're taking the most efficient route.

Auto-Rickshaw:

If possible, provide the auto-rickshaw driver with specific landmarks or major intersections to help them navigate. Avoid vague directions to prevent unnecessary detours.

Ride-Sharing:

Input your destination accurately on the ride-sharing app to ensure the driver follows the correct route. Monitor the route on the app during the journey to avoid any deviations.

- **Stay Alert and Aware**

Taxi:

Keep track of the meter during your journey to ensure the fare remains accurate. If you notice any discrepancies, politely address them with the driver.

Auto-Rickshaw:

Be wary of auto-rickshaw drivers who refuse to use the meter or insist on fixed fares. Politely decline such offers and opt for another vehicle.

Ride-Sharing:

Verify the vehicle details, including the license plate number and driver's name, before boarding the ride-sharing vehicle. This ensures you're entering the correct vehicle and driver details match the app.

- **Practice Safety Measures Taxi, Auto-Rickshaw, and Ride-Sharing:**

Share your trip details, including the vehicle details and estimated arrival time, with a trusted friend or family member. This adds an extra layer of security during your journey.

By following these tips, you can navigate Mumbai's bustling streets with confidence, ensuring a smooth and pleasant travel experience whether you're opting for a taxi, auto-rickshaw, or ride-sharing service.

Safety Tips and How to Avoid Common Scams

Mumbai is a bustling metropolis with a vibrant culture and welcoming populace. However, like any large city, it comes with its own set of challenges, including safety concerns and potential scams. Here are some safety tips and ways to avoid common scams, ensuring a pleasant and secure visit to Mumbai.

General Safety Tips

Stay Aware of Your Surroundings: Busy streets and crowded markets can be overwhelming. Keep your belongings close, and be cautious of pickpocketing, especially in crowded places like railway stations and popular tourist spots.

Use Reputable Transport Services: Opt for official taxi services or verified ride-sharing apps. Ensure the vehicle matches the details provided by the app, and share your trip details with someone you trust.

Respect Local Customs and Dress Appropriately: Mumbai is a cosmopolitan city with diverse cultures. Dressing conservatively, especially in religious sites and older parts of the city, is respectful and can help avoid unwanted attention.

Travel Insurance: It's wise to have travel insurance that covers theft, loss, and medical emergencies. Mumbai is generally safe, but it's better to be prepared for any situation.

Avoiding Common Scams

The Overpriced Taxi Ride: Always insist on using the meter in taxis. For auto-rickshaws and taxis without a digital meter, agree on a fare before starting your journey. Use GPS on your phone to ensure the driver is taking the correct route.

The Closed Attraction Scam: Be wary of individuals telling you that a major attraction is closed and offering to take you to another site or shop instead. This is often a ploy to guide you towards high-priced shops or tours. Always verify the information independently.

The Fake Official: Scammers may pose as police officers or government officials demanding to check your currency for counterfeits or asking for a fine. Always ask to see identification and, if in doubt, offer to settle any issues at the nearest police station.

Unofficial Tour Guides: At major tourist spots, you might be approached by unofficial tour guides offering their services. It's best to use guides recommended by your hotel or a reputable tour company to avoid being overcharged or misled.

The "Too Good to Be True" Offer: Be it shopping, dining, or entertainment, if an offer seems too good to be true, it probably is. Research or ask locals for recommendations to avoid being scammed with fake or overpriced goods and services.

Night Safety

Stay in Well-lit and Populated Areas: Mumbai's nightlife is vibrant, but it's important to stay in areas that are well-lit and crowded. Avoid dimly lit streets and deserted areas, especially if you're alone.

Use Trusted Transport: Late at night, rely on reputable taxi services or ride-sharing apps for transportation. Avoid walking long distances or using public transport late at night.

Inform Someone of Your Plans: Whether you're going out for the night or planning a day trip, let someone know your plans and expected return time.

Keeping Your Belongings Safe

Use Anti-theft Bags: Consider using anti-theft backpacks or bags with concealed zippers and RFID protection to carry your valuables.

Limit Cash and Valuables: Carry only what you need for the day. Use credit cards or digital payments where possible, and keep cash and valuables in a secure place.

Photocopy Important Documents: Keep a digital copy of important documents like your passport, visa, and ID in your email or secure cloud storage. Carry photocopies when exploring the city.

Following these tips can help you navigate Mumbai safely and enjoy all that this magnificent city has to offer without falling prey to common pitfalls or scams. Remember, awareness and preparation are key to a safe and enjoyable visit.

Chapter 4

Savor the Flavor: Dining and Cuisine

Street Food Galore: Must-Try Dishes

Mumbai, the bustling heart of India, is not just known for its fast-paced life or historic landmarks but also for a culinary landscape that's rich and diverse, especially when it comes to street food. Here's a guide to some must-try dishes that promise an explosion of flavors, along with recommendations on where to find them and an idea of how much they might cost.

Vada Pav at Anand Stall

Overview: Often dubbed the "Indian Burger," Vada Pav is Mumbai's signature street food. It consists of a spicy potato filling deep-fried in chickpea flour, nestled within a soft bread bun (pav), and served with an assortment of chutneys and fried green chilies.

Where to Try: Anand Stall, located near Mithibai College in Vile Parle, is famous for its Vada Pav. It's a hit among students and locals alike.

Cost: The cost per serving is around ₹20, making it an affordable yet filling snack.

Taste Experience: The combination of the soft bun, the spicy potato patty, and the tangy chutney offers a perfect balance of flavors and textures that can make anyone fall in love with Mumbai's street food.

Pav Bhaji at Cannon Pav Bhaji

Overview: Pav Bhaji is a spicy mixture of mashed vegetables cooked in a tomato-based gravy, served with butter-soaked pav. This dish is not only a taste sensation but also a complete meal.

Where to Try: Cannon Pav Bhaji, near CST station, is renowned for its rich and buttery Pav Bhaji.

Cost: A plate will cost you approximately ₹150, but the generous portions and the heavenly taste make it worth every penny.

Taste Experience: The buttery flavor of the pav paired with the spicy and tangy bhaji makes for an irresistible combination that epitomizes Mumbai's street food culture.

Bombay Sandwich at Amar Juice Centre

Overview: The Bombay Sandwich is a unique blend of the most unexpected ingredients – boiled potatoes, cucumber, beetroot, onion, tomato, mint chutney, and sometimes even slices of cheese, all sandwiched between buttered bread slices.

Where to Try: Amar Juice Centre, located near Cooper Hospital in Vile Parle, offers one of the best Bombay Sandwiches in the city.

Cost: You can enjoy this delightful sandwich for about ₹50.

Taste Experience: The freshness of the vegetables, the tanginess of the chutney, and the creaminess of the butter and cheese come together to create a refreshing yet hearty snack.

Pani Puri at Elco Pani Puri Centre

Overview: Pani Puri, also known as Golgappa or Phuchka in other parts of India, consists of hollow, crispy puris filled with a mixture of flavored water (pani), tamarind chutney, chili, chaat masala, potato, onion, and chickpeas.

Where to Try: Elco Pani Puri Centre, located on Hill Road in Bandra, is famous for its hygienic yet mouth-watering Pani Puri.

Cost: For around ₹60, you can get a plate of these little bombs of happiness.

Taste Experience: The burst of flavors from the spicy, tangy, and sweet water combined with the crunchy puri and the savory fillings is a true delight to the taste buds.

These iconic street foods not only reflect Mumbai's culinary diversity but also its welcoming spirit and vibrant culture. Each dish tells a story of the city's past and present, making them a must-try for anyone wanting to experience the essence of Mumbai.

Fine Dining in Mumbai: A Culinary Journey

Mumbai's culinary scene is as diverse as its population, with an array of fine dining restaurants that promise an unforgettable gastronomic journey. From the traditional flavors of India to innovative global cuisine, the city's fine dining landscape is vibrant and eclectic. Here are some of the top fine dining experiences in Mumbai, each offering not just exquisite food but an atmosphere to match.

Masque – An Ode to Modern Indian Cuisine

Overview: Nestled in the bustling area of Mahalaxmi, Masque is a culinary haven that focuses on farm-to-table dining, offering a 10-course tasting menu that changes with the seasons.

Cuisine: Modern Indian

Experience: The ambiance is as carefully curated as the menu, with an elegant and minimalist decor that allows the food to take center stage. Each dish is a work of art, presenting a unique blend of traditional Indian flavors with modern cooking techniques.

Cost: The 10-course chef's tasting menu costs approximately ₹4,000 per person, excluding drinks.

Signature Dish: The menu changes regularly, but look out for their innovative takes on classic dishes, such as Kashmiri morels with walnut dust.

Wasabi by Morimoto – Japanese Excellence

Overview: Located in the iconic Taj Mahal Palace Hotel, Wasabi by Morimoto offers an exquisite Japanese dining experience, brought to Mumbai by the legendary Iron Chef Masaharu Morimoto.

Cuisine: Japanese

Experience: The restaurant boasts a sleek, contemporary interior with views overlooking the Arabian Sea. The menu includes sushi, sashimi, and other Japanese specialties prepared with ingredients flown in from Japan.

Cost: Dining here can cost upwards of ₹5,000 per person, depending on your choice of dishes.

Signature Dish: The Toro Tartare, a dish made with the finest tuna belly, is a must-try.

Ziya – Contemporary Indian with a Twist

Overview: Under the guidance of Michelin-starred chef Vineet Bhatia, Ziya at The Oberoi, Mumbai, offers an innovative approach to Indian cuisine, with dishes that are both familiar and surprising.

Cuisine: Indian (Contemporary)

Experience: The restaurant offers stunning views of the ocean and features a gold-leaf ceiling, creating a luxurious dining atmosphere. The menu is a creative exploration of Indian cuisine, with each dish telling a story.

Cost: Expect to spend about ₹3,500 per person for a meal here.

Signature Dish: The lamb biryani, cooked with a unique blend of spices and served in a clay pot, is highly recommended.

Trèsind Mumbai – A Molecular Gastronomy Adventure

Overview: Bringing the avant-garde culinary techniques of molecular gastronomy to Indian cuisine, Trèsind Mumbai is a place where food and art converge.

Cuisine: Indian (Molecular Gastronomy)

Experience: Located in the bustling business district of Bandra Kurla Complex, Trèsind offers an intimate dining experience. The chefs play with textures, temperatures, and presentations to create dishes that are both innovative and deeply rooted in Indian culinary traditions.

Cost: A meal for two can cost around ₹6,000, making it a place for special occasions.

Signature Dish: The deconstructed pani puri and the smoked mutton chaap are standout dishes that perfectly embody the restaurant's innovative approach.

The Table – Globally Inspired Cuisine

Overview: Situated in Colaba, The Table has been a staple in Mumbai's fine dining scene, known for its globally inspired dishes made from locally sourced ingredients.

Cuisine: Global

Experience: The restaurant's split-level design, featuring a black and white marble bar on the ground floor and intimate dining spaces above, sets the stage for a relaxed yet refined dining experience. The menu is diverse, offering everything from zucchini spaghetti to Korean fried chicken.

Cost: Dining at The Table will cost around ₹3,000 to ₹4,000 per person.

Signature Dish: The Table's zucchini spaghetti, a healthier take on the classic dish, is both delicious and visually appealing.

These fine dining establishments not only highlight Mumbai's culinary diversity but also its capacity to blend tradition with innovation, offering diners not just a meal but a memorable journey through flavors, textures, and aromas. Whether you're a local or a traveler, dining at these spots promises to be a highlight of your Mumbai experience.

Vegetarian Delights: A Taste of Mumbai's Vegetarian Cuisine

Mumbai's culinary landscape is a paradise for vegetarian food lovers, offering a variety of dishes that are as diverse and vibrant as the city itself. From traditional Indian thalis to innovative vegetarian cafes, the city caters to every palate. Here's a glimpse into the vegetarian delights that make Mumbai a vegetarian's dream destination.

Shree Thaker Bhojanalay – The Quintessential Gujarati Thali

Overview: Nestled in the heart of Mumbai's bustling Kalbadevi area, Shree Thaker Bhojanalay is a legendary establishment known for its authentic Gujarati thalis.

Experience: Stepping into Shree Thaker Bhojanalay is like being welcomed into a Gujarati home. The unlimited thali includes a variety of dishes, such as fluffy rotis, creamy dal, savory vegetables, and sweet desserts, all served on a gleaming silver platter.

Cost: An unlimited thali costs approximately ₹800 per person, offering value for money given the variety and quality of dishes.

Signature Delight: The dal dhokli, a traditional Gujarati dish made from pieces of wheat dough cooked in a lentil curry, is a must-try.

Swati Snacks – Street Food with a Twist

Overview: Swati Snacks, located in Tardeo, is a contemporary eatery that brings traditional street food into a clean and comfortable setting, without compromising on the authentic flavors.

Experience: The ambiance is casual and inviting, making it a perfect spot for a quick bite or a leisurely meal. The menu features an array of snacks and main dishes, many of which are innovative takes on classic street food.

Cost: Prices are moderate, with snacks and main dishes ranging from ₹250 to ₹500.

Signature Delight: The Panki, a light snack made from rice flour batter cooked between banana leaves, is delicately flavored and melts in your mouth.

Bombay Salad Co. – Health Meets Taste

Overview: Bombay Salad Co. caters to the health-conscious crowd, offering a menu that's as nutritious as it is delicious, located in the trendy neighborhood of Bandra.

Experience: The chic and minimalist decor complements the healthy and vibrant offerings on the menu. You can create your own salad from a variety of fresh ingredients or choose from one of their expertly crafted combinations.

Cost: Salads and meals range from ₹400 to ₹700, reflecting the premium, fresh ingredients used.

Signature Delight: The Mediterranean Quinoa Salad, packed with flavors and nutrients, is a top pick for a light yet fulfilling meal.

Aharveda – Vegan Magic

Overview: Aharveda takes vegan dining to a whole new level, offering dishes that are not just meat-free but also avoid the use of sugar, oil, and processed ingredients, located in Andheri West.

Experience: The ambiance is simple and serene, focusing entirely on the holistic dining experience. The menu includes a variety of Indian and international dishes, all prepared in a way that maximizes nutritional value without sacrificing taste.

Cost: Meals are priced around ₹500 to ₹700, a fair trade for wholesome, nutritious dining.

Signature Delight: The vegan pizza, with its crispy base and flavorful topping of fresh vegetables and vegan cheese, is a revelation for those skeptical of dairy-free cheese.

Cafe Madras – South Indian Staples

Overview: A South Bombay institution, Cafe Madras serves up authentic South Indian cuisine that's both delicious and affordable, located in the King's Circle area of Matunga.

Experience: The cafe's no-frills ambiance takes you back in time, and the fast service ensures a steady stream of dosas, idlis, and vadas flying out of the kitchen.

Cost: It's hard to spend more than ₹300 per person here, making it an excellent value-for-money option.

Signature Delight: The Masala Dosa, crispy and filled with a flavorful potato mixture, served with coconut chutney and sambar, is iconic.

Mumbai's vegetarian cuisine reflects the city's diversity, offering flavors and dishes that span the breadth of India's culinary heritage. Whether you're seeking a lavish thali, a healthy salad, or a comforting dosa, Mumbai's vegetarian scene has something to delight every type of diner.

Food Tours and Cooking Classes: Immersive Culinary Experiences

For those looking to dive deep into the heart of Mumbai's culinary landscape, the city offers a plethora of immersive experiences. From guided food tours that navigate the bustling streets to intimate cooking classes hosted by local chefs, these experiences not only satiate your appetite but also provide a deeper understanding and appreciation of Mumbai's rich food culture.

Mumbai Street Food Tours

Overview: Embark on a gastronomic journey through Mumbai's lively streets, exploring the city's most famous food spots. These tours are perfect for adventurous eaters and cultural enthusiasts alike, offering a taste of Mumbai's iconic snacks and sweets.

Experience: Guided by local food experts, participants visit popular eateries and hidden gems, sampling a variety of dishes such as vada pav, bhel puri, and kulfi. Tours often include stops at historic landmarks, adding a layer of cultural exploration to the culinary adventure.

Cost: Prices vary depending on the tour provider and length of the tour, typically ranging from ₹1,500 to ₹3,000 per person.

Signature Experience: Trying the pav bhaji at a beachside stall as the sun sets, combining the flavors of Mumbai with its scenic beauty.

Home Cooking Classes

Overview: For a hands-on experience, nothing beats a home cooking class with a Mumbai local. These classes offer an intimate glimpse into the preparation of traditional Indian meals, from sourcing ingredients to the final touches that add flavor and aroma.

Experience: Participants are welcomed into the homes of local chefs or culinary enthusiasts, where they learn to cook a variety of dishes. Classes often end with a communal meal, where everyone sits down to enjoy the fruits of their labor.

Cost: Cooking classes can range from ₹2,000 to ₹5,000, depending on the menu and duration of the class.

Signature Experience: Learning to prepare a Maharashtrian thali, complete with dal, rice, vegetable curries, and chapati, offering a comprehensive look at regional cooking techniques.

Specialty Food Walks

Overview: Specialty food walks focus on a particular aspect of Mumbai's food scene, such as its bustling spice markets, the legacy of Parsi cafés, or the burgeoning organic food movement.

Experience: These walks are curated to offer a deeper dive into specific culinary traditions or trends. Participants might find themselves navigating the aromatic lanes of the spice market with an expert guide or savoring the unique flavors of Parsi cuisine at century-old cafés.

Cost: Specialty food walks can vary in price, generally falling between ₹1,500 and ₹3,500 per person, depending on the focus and duration.

Signature Experience: Visiting a Parsi café for an authentic berry pulao and mawa cake, experiencing the unique blend of Persian and Gujarati flavors that define Parsi cuisine.

Market Tours and Cooking Demonstrations

Overview: Market tours combined with cooking demonstrations offer a farm-to-table experience, showcasing the journey of ingredients from the bustling markets of Mumbai to a deliciously prepared dish.

Experience: Starting early in the morning, participants visit local markets to handpick fresh vegetables, spices, and other ingredients. Following the market tour, a cooking demonstration highlights how these ingredients are used in everyday Mumbai cooking.

Cost: These experiences generally cost between ₹2,500 and ₹4,500, providing insight into Mumbai's food ecosystem from market to meal.

Signature Experience: Selecting fresh seafood at the bustling Sassoon Dock and then learning to cook a traditional Malvani fish curry, experiencing the coastal flavors of Maharashtra.

Each of these culinary experiences offers a unique way to connect with Mumbai's food culture, providing memories that extend beyond the taste of the dishes. Whether you're exploring the streets on a food tour, getting hands-on in a cooking class, or diving into the specifics with a specialty walk, Mumbai's culinary scene promises to enrich and delight.

Chapter 5

After Dark: Exploring Mumbai's Nightlife

Clubs and Bars: Where to Enjoy Mumbai at Night

Mumbai's nightlife is vibrant and diverse, offering a plethora of clubs and bars catering to every taste and preference. Whether you're seeking pulsating dance floors, rooftop lounges with stunning views, or cozy neighborhood bars, Mumbai has it all. Here's a curated list of some of the best clubs and bars in the city, along with their locations, opening hours, and an overview of each establishment:

Trilogy Super Club

Location: Hotel Sea Princess, Juhu Tara Road, Juhu Beach, Mumbai.

Opening Hours: 9:00 PM to 1:30 AM (Closed on Mondays).

Overview: Situated in the heart of Juhu Beach, Trilogy Super Club is a high-energy nightclub known for its lively ambiance and top-notch DJ performances. With its futuristic decor, state-of-the-art sound system, and spacious dance floor, Trilogy attracts party-goers from all over the city. The club also offers VIP bottle service and exclusive lounge areas for those seeking a more upscale experience.

Aer - Four Seasons

Location: Four Seasons Hotel Mumbai, 1/136, Dr. E. Moses Road, Worli, Mumbai.

Opening Hours: 5:00 PM to 1:30 AM (Open daily).

Overview: Perched on the 34th floor of the Four Seasons Hotel, Aer offers unparalleled panoramic views of the Mumbai skyline. This stylish rooftop bar is renowned for its sophisticated ambiance, extensive cocktail menu, and upscale clientele. Whether you're enjoying sunset cocktails or dancing under the stars, Aer promises a memorable night out in the city.

Hoppipola

Location: 759, Ramee Guestline Hotel, A.B. Nair Road, Juhu, Mumbai.

Opening Hours: 12:00 PM to 1:30 AM (Open daily).

Overview: Hoppipola is a quirky and eclectic bar located in the vibrant neighborhood of Juhu. Known for its playful decor, casual vibe, and extensive selection of drinks, Hoppipola is the perfect spot for a laid-back night out with friends. The bar also offers board games, foosball tables, and other entertainment options to keep guests engaged throughout the evening.

Kitty Su

Location: The Lalit Mumbai, Sahar Airport Road, Mumbai.

Opening Hours: 10:00 PM to 3:00 AM (Open on Fridays and Saturdays).

Overview: Kitty Su is a glamorous nightclub located in The Lalit Mumbai hotel, known for its opulent interiors and world-class entertainment. With its resident DJs spinning the latest tracks, celebrity appearances, and themed parties, Kitty Su promises an unforgettable nightlife experience. The club also hosts drag shows, live performances, and other special events that add to its allure.

Colaba Social

Location: 24, Ground Floor, Glen Rose Building, Behind Taj Mahal Palace, Apollo Bunder, Colaba, Mumbai.

Opening Hours: 9:00 AM to 1:30 AM (Open daily).

Overview: Colaba Social is a trendy gastropub located in the heart of South Mumbai's Colaba neighborhood. Known for its hipster-chic ambiance, innovative cocktails, and fusion cuisine, Colaba Social attracts a young and eclectic crowd. Whether you're sipping on artisanal cocktails or indulging in comfort food favorites, Colaba Social offers a relaxed and welcoming atmosphere for guests to unwind after a long day.

Cultural Performances and Theatre: Nighttime Arts

Mumbai's cultural scene comes alive after the sun sets, with a plethora of performances and theatrical productions that showcase the city's rich artistic heritage. From traditional dance performances to avant-garde theater, there's something for every art enthusiast to enjoy. Here's a curated list of cultural performances and theaters in

Mumbai, along with their locations, opening hours, and an overview of each venue:

Prithvi Theatre

Location: 20, Janki Kutir, Juhu Church Road, Mumbai.

Opening Hours: Varies depending on scheduled performances.

Overview: Founded by the renowned actor and filmmaker Shashi Kapoor, Prithvi Theatre is a legendary cultural institution that has been at the forefront of Mumbai's theater scene for decades. Nestled in the charming neighborhood of Juhu, Prithvi Theatre hosts a diverse range of performances, including plays, musicals, stand-up comedy, and poetry readings. With its intimate setting and cozy ambiance, Prithvi Theatre offers a unique and immersive theater experience for audiences of all ages.

National Centre for the Performing Arts (NCPA)

Location: NCPA Marg, Nariman Point, Mumbai.

Opening Hours: Varies depending on scheduled performances.

Overview: Situated in the heart of Mumbai's business district, the National Centre for the Performing Arts (NCPA) is a premier cultural institution dedicated to showcasing the finest in music, dance, theater, and film. The NCPA boasts multiple venues, including the iconic Jamshed Bhabha Theatre and Tata Theatre, which host a diverse array of performances by both Indian and international artists. From classical concerts to contemporary dance productions, the NCPA offers a world-class cultural experience that is not to be missed.

Prithvi Cafe

Location: Inside Prithvi Theatre, 20, Janki Kutir, Juhu Church Road, Mumbai.

Opening Hours: 10:00 AM to 10:00 PM (Open daily).

Overview: Adjacent to Prithvi Theatre, Prithvi Cafe is a cozy and eclectic cafe that serves as a hub for artists and theater enthusiasts alike. Boasting a charming ambiance with rustic decor and outdoor seating, Prithvi Cafe offers a relaxed setting to unwind before or after a performance. The cafe serves a variety of snacks, beverages, and comfort food, making it the perfect spot for a casual meal or coffee date.

Ravindra Natya Mandir

Location: Prabhadevi, Mumbai.

Opening Hours: Varies depending on scheduled performances.

Overview: Ravindra Natya Mandir is a cultural complex dedicated to promoting and preserving Indian performing arts, located in the Prabhadevi area of Mumbai. The venue hosts a wide range of cultural events, including classical music concerts, dance recitals, theater productions, and film screenings. With its spacious auditoriums and state-of-the-art facilities, Ravindra Natya Mandir provides a platform for both established and emerging artists to showcase their talent.

The Drama School Mumbai

Location: 5th Floor, Mumbai Marathi Sahitya Sangh, Dr. Bhalerao Marg, Mumbai.

Opening Hours: Varies depending on scheduled workshops and performances.

Overview: The Drama School Mumbai is a pioneering institution dedicated to training aspiring actors and theater practitioners in the craft of theater. In addition to offering comprehensive training programs, The Drama School Mumbai also hosts regular performances, workshops, and masterclasses led by renowned theater professionals. From experimental theater to contemporary adaptations of classic plays, The Drama School

Mumbai fosters a vibrant and dynamic theater community in Mumbai.

Whether you're a theater aficionado or simply looking to immerse yourself in Mumbai's cultural scene, these venues offer a diverse array of performances and experiences that celebrate the arts in all its forms. From classic plays to avant-garde experiments, Mumbai's nighttime arts scene is sure to inspire and entertain audiences of all backgrounds.

Night Markets and Late-Night Eats: A Different Side of Mumbai

Mumbai's vibrancy doesn't fade when the sun sets; instead, it comes alive in the form of bustling night markets and tantalizing late-night eats. From savory street food to unique shopping experiences, exploring Mumbai after dark offers a glimpse into the city's nocturnal charm. Here's a curated list of night markets and late-night eateries in Mumbai, along with their locations, opening hours, and an overview of each spot:

Crawford Market

Location: Dhobi Talao, Chhatrapati Shivaji Maharaj Marg, Fort, Mumbai.

Opening Hours: 6:00 AM to 8:00 PM (closed on Sundays).

Overview: Crawford Market transforms into a bustling hub of activity after dark, with vendors setting up stalls selling everything from fresh produce to street food delicacies. As the night wears on, the market comes alive with the aroma of spicy snacks and the chatter of shoppers. Visitors can sample local street food favorites like pav bhaji, bhel puri, and vada pav while browsing through the eclectic array of goods on offer.

Mohammad Ali Road

Location: Mohammad Ali Road, Bhendi Bazaar, Mumbai.

Opening Hours: After sunset until late into the night, especially during the month of Ramadan.

Overview: Mohammad Ali Road is synonymous with Mumbai's vibrant street food culture, particularly during the holy month of Ramadan. After sunset, the bustling thoroughfare transforms into a food lover's paradise, with vendors lining the streets offering an array of savory and sweet treats.

From succulent kebabs and fragrant biryanis to rich desserts like malpua and falooda, Mohammad Ali Road is a must-visit destination for late-night foodies.

Linking Road Night Market

Location: Linking Road, Bandra West, Mumbai.

Opening Hours: 10:00 PM to 4:00 AM (open on Fridays and Saturdays).

Overview: Linking Road Night Market offers a unique shopping experience for those looking to indulge in some late-night retail therapy. The market comes alive after dark, with vendors selling a variety of clothing, accessories, and handicrafts at bargain prices. Visitors can browse through the stalls while sampling street food snacks like grilled sandwiches, kebabs, and fresh fruit juices, making it a popular spot for both locals and tourists alike.

Bade Miyan

Location: Tulloch Road, Apollo Bandar, Colaba, Mumbai.

Opening Hours: 7:00 PM to 2:00 AM (open daily).

Overview: Bade Miyan is a legendary late-night eatery in Mumbai, renowned for its mouthwatering kebabs and grilled delicacies. Tucked away in the bustling streets of Colaba, this humble eatery attracts a diverse crowd of food enthusiasts craving flavorful dishes served hot off the grill. From succulent seekh kebabs to juicy tandoori chicken, Bade Miyan promises a satisfying culinary experience that's perfect for late-night cravings.

Juhu Beach Food Stalls

Location: Juhu Beach, Juhu, Mumbai.

Opening Hours: Open until late into the night.

Overview: Juhu Beach is not just a popular destination for sunbathing and leisurely strolls; it's also a hotspot for late-night food stalls offering a variety of street food delights. As the evening progresses, the beach comes alive with the sizzle of grills and the aroma of fried snacks. Visitors can feast on favorites like corn on the cob, pav bhaji, and gola while enjoying the sea breeze and lively atmosphere.

Exploring Mumbai's night markets and late-night eateries offers a unique perspective on the city's culinary and cultural landscape. Whether you're sampling street food delicacies or hunting for bargains at a night market, these experiences promise to immerse you in the vibrant energy of Mumbai after dark.

Safety Tips for Night Owls

While exploring Mumbai's vibrant nightlife can be exhilarating, it's essential to prioritize safety to ensure a memorable and worry-free experience. Whether you're out late enjoying the city's cultural offerings or sampling street food at night markets, here are some safety tips for night owls in Mumbai:

Stick to Well-Lit Areas

When walking around at night, stick to well-lit streets and avoid dimly lit or secluded areas, especially if you're alone. Plan your route in advance and stay on main roads with a steady flow of pedestrian and vehicle traffic.

Travel in Groups

Whenever possible, travel with friends or in groups, as there is safety in numbers.

If you're attending a late-night event or exploring the city's nightlife, designate a meeting point in case you get separated from your group.

Use Licensed Transportation

Opt for licensed taxis, auto-rickshaws, or ride-sharing services when traveling at night.

Verify that the vehicle matches the details provided by the transportation app, and always share your trip details with a trusted friend or family member.

Keep Valuables Secure

Avoid carrying large sums of cash or wearing expensive jewelry when out at night.

Keep your belongings secure and close to your body, especially in crowded areas or on public transportation.

Stay Sober

Limit alcohol consumption and avoid using substances that impair your judgment or reaction time.

Stay hydrated and be mindful of your surroundings to ensure you can react quickly to any potential threats.

Stay Connected

Keep your phone fully charged and have emergency contacts saved in your phone.

Check in with friends or family members periodically to let them know your whereabouts and ensure your safety.

Plan Your Return Journey

Before heading out for the night, plan your return journey and familiarize yourself with transportation options available during late hours.

Avoid waiting alone at deserted bus stops or train stations, and consider pre-arranging a ride home if necessary.

Be Respectful

Respect local customs and cultural norms, especially when visiting religious sites or participating in cultural events.

Avoid engaging in confrontations or arguments with locals, and always be courteous and polite.

Know Emergency Numbers

Save important emergency numbers, such as the local police station and ambulance service, in your phone for quick access in case of an emergency.

Whether you're exploring the city's cultural offerings or indulging in late-night eats, prioritizing safety is key to having a memorable and enjoyable experience in Mumbai after dark.

Chapter 6

Must-Visit Attractions in Mumbai

The Gateway of India: A Symbolic Arch

The Gateway of India stands tall and majestic at the waterfront of Mumbai, serving as an iconic symbol of the city's rich history and cultural heritage. Built in the early 20th century during the British Raj, this architectural marvel has witnessed the ebb and flow of time, becoming a beloved landmark that welcomes visitors from across the globe.

Overview:

Designed in Indo-Saracenic style, the Gateway of India is a breathtaking fusion of architectural elements, featuring intricate latticework, ornamental flourishes, and towering minarets. Its grandeur and imposing presence make it a popular backdrop for tourists and locals alike, offering a stunning setting for photographs and leisurely strolls along the waterfront.

Historical Significance:

Constructed to commemorate the landing of King George V and Queen Mary in Mumbai in 1911, the Gateway of India holds immense historical significance. It witnessed the departure of the British troops from India in 1948, marking the end of British rule and the dawn of India's independence. Today, it stands as a poignant reminder of the nation's struggle for freedom and its enduring spirit of resilience.

Architectural Marvel:

The Gateway of India's imposing structure is adorned with intricate carvings and embellishments, showcasing the craftsmanship of Indian artisans during the colonial era. Its central dome is crowned with a sculpture of a seated figure representing Progress, while its four turrets symbolize the different communities of India. The archway itself is flanked by intricately sculpted panels depicting scenes from Indian mythology and history, adding to its visual allure.

Prominent Landmark:

As one of Mumbai's most prominent landmarks, the Gateway of India serves as a bustling hub of activity, attracting throngs of visitors throughout the year.

From leisurely promenades along the waterfront to boat rides to the nearby Elephanta Caves, the area surrounding the Gateway offers a myriad of recreational opportunities for tourists and locals alike.

Cost and Duration:

Visiting the Gateway of India is free of charge, making it accessible to all. The duration of your visit can vary depending on your interests and activities. A leisurely stroll around the monument and along the waterfront may take around 30 minutes to an hour, while exploring nearby attractions such as the Taj Mahal Palace Hotel or taking a boat ride to Elephanta Caves can extend your visit to several hours.

Accessibility:

Situated in the Colaba area of South Mumbai, the Gateway of India is easily accessible by various modes of transportation. Visitors can reach the monument by taxi, auto-rickshaw, or public bus. Additionally, the nearby Churchgate and Chhatrapati Shivaji Maharaj Terminus railway stations provide convenient access for those traveling by train.

The Chhatrapati Shivaji Maharaj Terminus: Architectural Marvel

The Chhatrapati Shivaji Maharaj Terminus, formerly known as the Victoria Terminus, stands as a majestic testament to Mumbai's rich architectural heritage and historical significance. This iconic railway station, a UNESCO World Heritage Site, is not merely a transportation hub but a masterpiece of Victorian Gothic architecture that captivates visitors with its grandeur and intricacy.

Overview:

Built in the late 19th century, the Chhatrapati Shivaji Maharaj Terminus is a stunning blend of Victorian, Gothic, and Indian architectural styles. Its imposing facade features towering turrets, ornate carvings, and exquisite stained glass windows, making it a visual spectacle that transports visitors back in time to the era of British colonial rule.

Historical Significance:

Originally commissioned to commemorate Queen Victoria's Golden

Jubilee, the Chhatrapati Shivaji Maharaj Terminus played a pivotal role in India's railway history and independence movement. It served as a crucial transportation hub for the British Raj and witnessed significant events, including the arrival of Mahatma Gandhi on his return from South Africa and the historic declaration of India's independence in 1947.

Architectural Marvel:

The architectural brilliance of the Chhatrapati Shivaji Maharaj Terminus is evident in every detail of its design. Its soaring dome, intricate spires, and ornamental friezes pay homage to the grandeur of Victorian architecture, while its fusion of Indian motifs and materials adds a unique touch of local flavor.

Inside, the station's vast concourse is adorned with decorative elements inspired by Hindu and Islamic art, creating a harmonious blend of cultures and traditions.

Prominent Landmark:

Beyond its functional role as a railway station, the Chhatrapati Shivaji Maharaj Terminus has become a symbol of Mumbai's identity and pride. Its bustling platforms, bustling corridors, and bustling ambiance reflect the energy and diversity of the city, while its iconic silhouette graces postcards, paintings, and photographs, symbolizing Mumbai's spirit of resilience and progress.

Cost and Duration:

Visiting the Chhatrapati Shivaji Maharaj Terminus is free of charge, allowing visitors to marvel at its architectural splendor at their leisure. The duration of your visit can vary depending on your interests and activities. Exploring the station's exterior and admiring its architectural details may take around 30 minutes to an hour, while a guided tour of its interiors and historical exhibits can extend your visit to several hours.

Accessibility:

Situated in the heart of Mumbai's Fort area, the Chhatrapati Shivaji Maharaj Terminus is easily accessible by various modes of transportation. The station is served by local trains, buses, taxis, and auto-rickshaws, making it convenient for visitors to reach from any part of the city. Additionally, the station's central location provides easy access to nearby attractions such as the Crawford Market, St. Xavier's College, and the Bombay High Court.

Marine Drive: Mumbai's Seaside Promenade

Marine Drive, also known as the Queen's Necklace, is an iconic stretch of coastline that epitomizes the essence of Mumbai's vibrant spirit and cosmopolitan charm. This picturesque promenade, flanked by palm trees and glittering skyscrapers, offers a serene escape from the hustle and bustle of the city, inviting visitors to relax, unwind, and soak in the breathtaking views of the Arabian Sea.

Overview:

Stretching along the shoreline of South Mumbai, Marine Drive is a 3.6-kilometer-long boulevard that curves gracefully along the Arabian Sea. Its distinctive C-shape and dazzling row of streetlights resemble a string of pearls when viewed from a distance, earning it the nickname "Queen's Necklace" due to its sparkling appearance at night.

Scenic Beauty:

Marine Drive is renowned for its stunning panoramic views of the Arabian Sea, especially during sunrise and sunset when the sky is ablaze with hues of orange and pink. The gentle sea breeze, rhythmic sound of waves, and breathtaking skyline create a serene and romantic ambiance that enchants visitors and locals alike.

Recreational Activities:

Marine Drive offers ample opportunities for leisure and recreation, with wide pedestrian pathways perfect for jogging, cycling, or simply strolling along the waterfront. Visitors can also relax on the numerous benches scattered along the promenade, savoring the cool sea breeze and watching as fishing boats and luxury yachts glide across the horizon.

Iconic Landmarks:

Several iconic landmarks dot the landscape of Marine Drive, including the elegant Art Deco buildings of the 1930s that line its southern end, such as the Rajabai Clock Tower and the InterContinental Hotel. At the northern end stands the famous Taraporewala Aquarium, where visitors can explore a diverse array of marine life.

Cost and Duration:

Visiting Marine Drive is free of charge, making it accessible to all. The duration of your visit can vary depending on your interests and activities. A leisurely stroll along the promenade may take around 30 minutes to an hour, while enjoying recreational activities or admiring the views can extend your visit to several hours.

Accessibility:

Situated in the heart of South Mumbai, Marine Drive is easily accessible by various modes of transportation. Visitors can reach the promenade by taxi, auto-rickshaw, or public bus from any part of the city. Additionally, the Marine Lines and Churchgate railway stations provide convenient access for those traveling by train.

Elephanta Caves: A UNESCO World Heritage Site

The Elephanta Caves, nestled on Elephanta Island in Mumbai Harbor, stand as a testament to India's rich cultural and artistic heritage. Designated as a UNESCO World Heritage Site, these ancient rock-cut caves are renowned for their magnificent sculptures, intricate carvings, and spiritual significance, attracting visitors from around the world to marvel at their timeless beauty and historical significance.

Overview:

The Elephanta Caves, also known as Gharapuri Caves, date back to the 5th to 8th centuries AD and comprise a complex of cave temples dedicated primarily to the Hindu god Shiva. The main cave, also known as the Great Cave, features a stunning array of rock-cut sculptures and reliefs depicting various aspects of Hindu mythology, including Shiva in his different forms and manifestations.

Historical and Spiritual Significance:

The Elephanta Caves hold immense historical and spiritual significance, serving as a sacred pilgrimage site for devotees of Lord Shiva. The intricate sculptures and reliefs found within the caves offer insights into ancient Indian art, culture, and religious practices, providing a glimpse into the spiritual beliefs and artistic achievements of bygone eras.

Architectural Marvel:

The architecture of the Elephanta Caves is a remarkable feat of ancient engineering and craftsmanship. Carved entirely out of solid basalt rock, the caves feature intricately sculpted columns, ornate pillars, and majestic statues that showcase the mastery of the artisans who created them. The most famous sculpture within the caves is the colossal three-headed bust of Shiva, known as Maheshamurti, which stands as a pinnacle of Indian rock-cut architecture.

Exploring the Caves:

Visitors to the Elephanta Caves can explore the various chambers and halls of the main cave, each adorned with stunning sculptures and reliefs depicting scenes from Hindu mythology. Highlights include the iconic Trimurti sculpture of Shiva, Vishnu, and Brahma, as well as depictions of Shiva in his many forms, including Nataraja (the cosmic dancer) and Ardhanarishvara (the half-male, half-female deity).

Cost and Duration:

Access to the Elephanta Caves involves a ferry ride from the Gateway of India to Elephanta Island, followed by a short hike or toy train ride up to the cave complex. The cost of the ferry ride and entrance fee to the caves varies depending on the type of ticket purchased. The duration of a visit to the Elephanta Caves typically ranges from 2 to 3 hours, allowing ample time to explore the caves and soak in their architectural and artistic splendor.

Accessibility:

The Elephanta Caves are accessible via ferry from the Gateway of India, with boats departing regularly throughout the day. The ferry ride takes approximately one hour each way, offering scenic views of Mumbai Harbor and the surrounding coastline. Once on Elephanta Island, visitors can explore the caves on foot or opt for a ride on the island's toy train.

Chapter 7

Day Trips and Excursions

Alibaug: Beach Bliss

As I step onto the sun-kissed shores of Alibaug, a sense of tranquility washes over me, accompanied by the gentle melody of waves lapping against the shoreline. Nestled along the Konkan coast of Maharashtra, Alibaug beckons with its pristine beaches, lush coconut groves, and laid-back charm, offering the perfect escape from the hustle and bustle of city life.

Morning Exploration:

The day begins with a leisurely stroll along the golden sands of Alibaug Beach, as the morning sun casts a warm glow over the tranquil waters of the Arabian Sea. I take in the panoramic views of the coastline, dotted with colorful fishing boats and swaying palm trees, feeling a sense of serenity envelop me as I breathe in the salty sea air.

Adventure Awaits:

Eager to explore further, I embark on an exhilarating boat ride to the historic Kolaba Fort, located just a short distance offshore. As the boat glides through the azure waters, I marvel at the imposing walls and bastions of the fort, which stand as a silent sentinel against the backdrop of the sea. Stepping onto the weathered stone ramparts, I am transported back in time, imagining the tales of bygone battles and maritime conquests that echo through its ancient corridors.

Cultural Immersion:

Returning to the mainland, I venture into the heart of Alibaug town to explore its rich cultural heritage. Wandering through the narrow lanes lined with quaint cottages and vibrant bazaars, I encounter the bustling markets where locals barter for fresh produce and handmade crafts. I pause to admire the ornate architecture of the historic temples and mosques that dot the landscape, each bearing testament to the region's diverse religious traditions.

Beachside Indulgence:

As the sun reaches its zenith, I seek refuge from the midday heat beneath the shade of a swaying palm tree, indulging in a picnic lunch of local delicacies sourced from the nearby markets. Savoring the flavors of fresh seafood and tropical fruits, I relish the simple pleasures of beachside dining, with the sound of laughter and conversation mingling with the rhythmic sound of waves.

Afternoon Retreat:

In the afternoon, I retreat to the tranquil confines of my beachside resort, where I am greeted by the soothing sound of rustling palm fronds and the scent of fragrant flowers. I take a refreshing dip in the crystal-clear waters of the resort's infinity pool, feeling the cares of the world melt away as I bask in the warmth of the afternoon sun.

Sunset Serenade:

As evening approaches, I make my way back to Alibaug Beach to witness the breathtaking spectacle of the sunset. With hues of crimson and gold painting the sky, I find a secluded spot on the sand to watch nature's masterpiece unfold before my eyes, feeling a sense of awe and wonder at the beauty of the world around me.

As I bid farewell to Alibaug, my heart is filled with gratitude for the unforgettable memories and moments of serenity that I have experienced in this coastal paradise. From the tranquil beaches to the historic forts and vibrant culture, Alibaug has captured my imagination and left an indelible mark on my soul, reminding me of the simple joys and timeless beauty that await those who dare to explore its shores.

Lonavala and Khandala: Hill Stations Near Mumbai

As I take a journey to the picturesque hill stations of Lonavala and Khandala, nestled amidst the lush greenery of the Western Ghats, I feel a sense of anticipation and excitement building within me. Located just a few hours' drive from the bustling metropolis of Mumbai, these charming retreats offer a refreshing escape from the chaos of city life, promising breathtaking vistas, serene landscapes, and a plethora of outdoor adventures waiting to be discovered.

Morning Exploration:

The day begins with a scenic drive through winding mountain roads, as verdant valleys and cascading waterfalls greet me at every turn. Arriving in Lonavala, I am immediately captivated by the serene beauty of the landscape, with mist-clad hills and emerald forests stretching out as far as the eye can see. My first stop is the iconic Tiger's Point, where I am rewarded with panoramic views of the surrounding valleys and ravines, shrouded in a mystical veil of morning mist.

Adventure Awaits:

Eager to explore further, I set out on a trek to the ancient Karla Caves, nestled amidst dense foliage and towering cliffs. As I ascend the stone steps leading to the caves, I am mesmerized by the intricate carvings and rock-cut sculptures that adorn the ancient walls, offering a glimpse into India's rich cultural heritage. Reaching the summit, I am treated to breathtaking views of the lush countryside below, with the cool mountain breeze invigorating my senses.

Cultural Immersion:

After a morning of adventure, I venture into the heart of Lonavala town to immerse myself in its rich cultural heritage. Wandering through the bustling streets lined with quaint shops and cafes, I encounter the vibrant local market, where vendors peddle a colorful array of handicrafts, spices, and traditional sweets. I pause to admire the ornate architecture of the historic temples and colonial-era buildings that dot the landscape, each bearing witness to the region's storied past.

Hill Station Indulgence:

As the day progresses, I make my way to Khandala, Lonavala's sister hill station, renowned for its cool climate and verdant landscapes. Nestled amidst mist-covered hills, Khandala offers a tranquil retreat from the hustle and bustle of city life, with sprawling tea estates and fragrant spice plantations dotting the landscape. I indulge in a leisurely stroll through the town's scenic vistas, pausing to savor the aroma of fresh mountain air and the sight of colorful flowers in bloom.

Afternoon Retreat:

In the afternoon, I retreat to a cozy hillside café overlooking the valley, where I indulge in a sumptuous feast of local delicacies and piping hot chai. As I relax in the shade of swaying palm trees, I am serenaded by the melodious chirping of birds and the rustle of leaves in the gentle breeze, feeling a sense of peace and contentment wash over me.

Sunset Serenade:

As evening approaches, I make my way to the scenic viewpoints of Sunset Point, where I am treated to a mesmerizing display of colors as the sun dips below the horizon, casting a warm glow over the verdant hills and valleys below. With hues of crimson and gold painting the sky, I find myself lost in the beauty of the moment, grateful for the opportunity to witness nature's masterpiece unfold before my eyes.

Matheran: A Vehicle-Free Hill Station Experience

As I set out on a journey to Matheran, the quaint hill station nestled in the Sahyadri range of Maharashtra, I am filled with a sense of anticipation for the unique adventure that awaits. Unlike its bustling counterparts, Matheran prides itself on being a vehicle-free zone, offering visitors a rare opportunity to experience the pristine beauty of nature in its purest form, free from the noise and pollution of modern transportation.

Morning Exploration:

The day begins with a scenic train ride from Neral to Matheran, a journey that takes me back in time as the century-old toy train chugs along the narrow gauge railway track, traversing lush forests and meandering streams. As the train ascends the steep slopes of the Western Ghats, I am treated to breathtaking views of the surrounding landscape, with mist-clad hills and verdant valleys stretching out as far as the eye can see.

Adventure Awaits:

Arriving in Matheran, I am greeted by the refreshing scent of eucalyptus and pine, as well as the soothing sounds of birdsong and rustling leaves. With no motorized vehicles allowed within its limits, I set out on foot to explore the town's myriad trails and pathways, each offering a new adventure and a chance to connect with nature. From gentle forest walks to challenging treks up rocky slopes, Matheran offers something for outdoor enthusiasts of all skill levels.

Cultural Immersion:

Wandering through the quaint streets of Matheran town, I am enchanted by its old-world charm and colonial-era architecture, with charming cottages and bungalows nestled amidst lush greenery. The town's bustling market is a treasure trove of local handicrafts, souvenirs, and delectable treats, offering a glimpse into the vibrant culture and traditions of the region.

Hill Station Indulgence:

As the day progresses, I retreat to one of Matheran's idyllic viewpoints to soak in the panoramic vistas of the surrounding landscape. From the sweeping vistas of

Echo Point to the tranquil beauty of Charlotte Lake, each viewpoint offers a new perspective on the natural splendor of the Sahyadri range, with the cool mountain breeze invigorating my senses and rejuvenating my spirit.

Afternoon Retreat:

In the afternoon, I seek refuge from the midday heat beneath the shade of a sprawling banyan tree, where I indulge in a leisurely picnic lunch of local delicacies and refreshing beverages. Surrounded by the sights and sounds of nature, I feel a sense of peace and contentment wash over me, grateful for the opportunity to escape the chaos of city life and reconnect with the simple pleasures of the outdoors.

Sunset Serenade:

As evening approaches, I make my way to one of Matheran's secluded viewpoints to witness the breathtaking spectacle of the sunset. With hues of gold and crimson painting the sky, I find myself lost in the beauty of the moment, as the sun dips below the horizon and casts a warm glow over the landscape below. In that tranquil moment, I am reminded of the timeless beauty and serenity that await those who venture off the beaten path and embrace the natural wonders of Matheran.

The Kanheri Caves: Ancient Buddhist Caves

Embarking on a journey to the Kanheri Caves, nestled within the Sanjay Gandhi National Park in Mumbai, I am filled with a sense of reverence for the rich history and spiritual significance of these ancient rock-cut monuments. Carved out of the basalt cliffs centuries ago, the Kanheri Caves stand as a testament to the enduring legacy of Buddhism in the region, offering visitors a glimpse into the lives of monks and pilgrims who once sought solace and enlightenment within their hallowed halls.

Morning Exploration:

As the sun rises over the dense forests of the national park, I make my way along the winding pathways that lead to the entrance of the Kanheri Caves. The tranquil surroundings and chirping birdsong create a serene ambiance, setting the stage for a journey back in time to a bygone era of spiritual enlightenment and artistic expression.

Ancient Artistry:

Entering the caves, I am immediately struck by the intricate carvings and sculptures that adorn the rock-cut facades, depicting scenes from the life of the Buddha, as well as mythological figures and celestial beings. The craftsmanship and attention to detail are awe-inspiring, with each carving telling a story and inviting contemplation on the nature of existence and the pursuit of inner peace.

Spiritual Sanctuary:

Exploring the labyrinthine chambers and halls of the Kanheri Caves, I am drawn to the peaceful atmosphere that pervades the ancient sanctuary. The cool, dimly lit interiors offer respite from the heat of the day, while the rhythmic chanting of Buddhist prayers echoes through the corridors, transporting me to a state of deep meditation and reflection.

Cultural Immersion:

As I wander through the caves, I encounter numerous inscriptions and graffiti left behind by pilgrims and visitors from centuries past, each bearing witness to the enduring legacy of the site as a place of pilgrimage and worship. From simple etchings to elaborate murals, these ancient markings offer insights into the beliefs and customs of the people who once inhabited these sacred spaces.

Hillside Haven:

Emerging from the caves, I am greeted by sweeping views of the surrounding landscape, with verdant hills and dense forests stretching out as far as the eye can see. Finding a secluded spot amidst the rocky outcrops, I take a moment to soak in the natural beauty of the surroundings, feeling a deep sense of connection to the earth and all living beings.

Afternoon Reflection:

As the day progresses, I find a shady spot beneath a towering tree to rest and reflect on my journey through the Kanheri Caves. Surrounded by the sights and sounds of nature, I feel a sense of peace and tranquility wash over me, grateful for the opportunity to experience the profound spirituality and ancient wisdom that permeate this sacred site.

Chapter 8

Museums and Galleries

The Chhatrapati Shivaji Maharaj Vastu Sangrahalaya: Art and History

Nestled in the heart of Mumbai, the Chhatrapati Shivaji Maharaj Vastu Sangrahalaya (formerly known as the Prince of Wales Museum) stands as a beacon of culture and heritage, showcasing a rich tapestry of art, history, and craftsmanship from India and beyond. This iconic institution, housed within a majestic Indo-Saracenic building, offers visitors a captivating journey through the annals of time, providing insights into the diverse cultures and civilizations that have shaped the Indian subcontinent.

Exploring the Collections:

As I step through the grand entrance of the museum, I am greeted by an impressive array of artifacts and antiquities spanning thousands of years of human history. From ancient sculptures and artifacts dating back to the Indus Valley Civilization to exquisite miniature paintings and intricately crafted textiles from the Mughal era, the museum's diverse collections offer a comprehensive overview of India's artistic and cultural heritage.

Location and Hours:

Located in the historic precinct of Kala Ghoda in South Mumbai, the Chhatrapati Shivaji Maharaj Vastu

Sangrahalaya is easily accessible by public transportation, with ample parking facilities available nearby. The museum is open to visitors from Tuesday to Sunday, from 10:15 AM to 6:00 PM, with extended hours on certain days for special exhibitions and events. Admission fees vary depending on the visitor's age and nationality, with discounted rates available for students, seniors, and groups.

Architectural Marvel:

The museum's imposing facade, with its intricately carved arches, domes, and minarets, is a masterpiece of Indo-Saracenic architecture, reminiscent of the grandeur of India's medieval palaces and forts. Designed by renowned architect George Wittet and completed in 1922, the building itself is a work of art, blending elements of Indian, Islamic, and British architectural styles to create a truly unique and captivating aesthetic.

Highlights of the Collection:

Among the museum's most prized possessions is the exquisite Jade Gallery, showcasing rare jade carvings and artifacts from China, Central Asia, and India. The Natural History section, with its extensive collection of fossils, minerals, and taxidermy specimens, offers a fascinating glimpse into the natural world. The Arms and Armor Gallery, featuring ancient weapons and armor from various Indian dynasties, is a testament to the martial prowess and craftsmanship of bygone eras.

Guided Tours and Workshops:

For a deeper understanding of the museum's collections, visitors can participate in guided tours led by knowledgeable curators and experts, who offer insights into the historical and cultural significance of each exhibit. The museum also hosts regular workshops, lectures, and cultural events, providing opportunities for visitors to engage with artists, scholars, and historians and delve deeper into their areas of interest.

The National Gallery of Modern Art: Contemporary Insights

Located in the heart of Mumbai, the National Gallery of Modern Art (NGMA) stands as a bastion of contemporary art, offering visitors a dynamic and immersive experience that celebrates the vibrant creativity of Indian artists. With its diverse collection of paintings, sculptures, installations, and multimedia artworks, the NGMA provides a window into the ever-evolving landscape of modern Indian art, showcasing the talents and perspectives of both established masters and emerging talents.

Exploring the Collections:

Stepping into the hallowed halls of the NGMA, I am immediately struck by the kaleidoscope of colors and forms that adorn the gallery walls. From bold abstract canvases to thought-provoking conceptual installations, the museum's eclectic collection reflects the myriad influences and inspirations that shape the contemporary Indian art scene. Each artwork tells a story, offering insights into the social, cultural, and political forces that shape our world today.

Location and Hours:

Situated in Colaba, South Mumbai, the NGMA is conveniently located near other cultural landmarks and attractions, making it easily accessible by public transportation or car. The gallery is open to visitors from Tuesday to Sunday, from 11:00 AM to 6:00 PM, with extended hours on certain days for special exhibitions and events. Admission fees vary depending on the visitor's age and nationality, with discounted rates available for students, seniors, and groups.

Exhibition Highlights:

One of the highlights of the NGMA's collection is its extensive holdings of works by renowned Indian artists such as M.F. Husain, Tyeb Mehta, F.N. Souza, and Amrita Sher-Gil. The museum also features rotating exhibitions that showcase the latest trends and developments in contemporary Indian art, providing a platform for emerging artists to showcase their talents and engage with the public.

Interactive Experiences:

In addition to its permanent and temporary exhibitions, the NGMA offers a range of interactive experiences and educational programs designed to engage visitors of all ages. From guided tours and artist talks to hands-on workshops and film screenings, the museum provides opportunities for visitors to deepen their understanding of contemporary art and explore their own creativity.

Café and Bookstore:

After immersing myself in the world of contemporary art, I take a moment to relax and unwind at the NGMA's café, where I indulge in a refreshing beverage and delicious snack amidst the tranquil surroundings of the museum. Nearby, the museum's bookstore offers a curated selection of art books, catalogs, and souvenirs, allowing me to take home a piece of the NGMA experience.

Dr. Bhau Daji Lad Mumbai City Museum: Mumbai's Rich Heritage

Nestled in the heart of Mumbai's bustling Byculla neighborhood, the Dr. Bhau Daji Lad Mumbai City Museum stands as a testament to the city's rich cultural heritage and storied past. Housed within a majestic Victorian-era building, this iconic institution offers visitors a captivating journey through the history, art, and culture of Mumbai, showcasing the diverse traditions and influences that have shaped the metropolis into the vibrant and dynamic city it is today.

Exploring the Collections:

Stepping through the grand entrance of the museum, I am greeted by a treasure trove of artifacts, artworks, and historical memorabilia that span centuries of Mumbai's history. From ancient artifacts and archaeological finds to colonial-era maps and photographs, the museum's diverse collections provide insights into the city's evolution from a humble fishing village to a bustling cosmopolitan metropolis.

Location and Hours:

Conveniently located near the Byculla Zoo and other cultural attractions, the Dr. Bhau Daji Lad Mumbai City Museum is easily accessible by public transportation or car. The museum is open to visitors from Tuesday to Sunday, from 10:00 AM to 6:00 PM, with extended hours on certain days for special exhibitions and events.

Admission fees vary depending on the visitor's age and nationality, with discounted rates available for students, seniors, and groups.

Architectural Marvel:

The museum's historic building, originally known as the Victoria and Albert Museum, is a masterpiece of Victorian-era architecture, with its elegant domes, intricate carvings, and ornate galleries evoking the grandeur of Mumbai's colonial past. Designed by renowned architect George Wittet and completed in 1872, the building itself is a work of art, serving as a fitting backdrop for the museum's rich collections.

Highlights of the Collection:

Among the museum's most prized possessions are its collection of decorative arts and crafts, including exquisite textiles, ceramics, and metalwork from various periods of Mumbai's history. The museum also features rotating exhibitions that highlight specific aspects of the city's culture and heritage, offering visitors a deeper understanding of Mumbai's diverse communities and traditions.

Interactive Experiences:

In addition to its permanent and temporary exhibitions, the Dr. Bhau Daji Lad Mumbai City Museum offers a range of interactive experiences and educational programs designed to engage visitors of all ages. From guided tours and workshops to film screenings and cultural performances, the museum provides opportunities for visitors to connect with Mumbai's rich heritage in meaningful and immersive ways.

Café and Gift Shop:

After exploring the museum's galleries and exhibitions, I take a moment to relax and recharge at the museum's café, where I enjoy a cup of chai and a light snack amidst the tranquil surroundings of the museum courtyard. Nearby, the museum's gift shop offers a curated selection of books, souvenirs, and handicrafts inspired by Mumbai's rich cultural heritage, allowing me to take home a memento of my visit.

The Jehangir Art Gallery: A Hub for Modern Art

Located in the heart of Mumbai's vibrant art district, the Jehangir Art Gallery stands as a beacon of creativity and innovation, showcasing the best of contemporary Indian art to visitors from around the world. Established in 1952, this iconic institution has played a pivotal role in nurturing and promoting the talents of emerging artists, as well as showcasing the works of established masters, making it a must-visit destination for art enthusiasts and culture aficionados alike.

Exploring the Galleries:

Stepping into the hallowed halls of the Jehangir Art Gallery, I am immediately struck by the energy and dynamism that permeate the space. The gallery's diverse collection of paintings, sculptures, and mixed media works span a wide range of styles and genres, from abstract expressionism to figurative realism, providing visitors with a comprehensive overview of the contemporary Indian art scene.

Location and Hours:

Conveniently situated in the Kala Ghoda neighborhood of South Mumbai, the Jehangir Art Gallery is easily accessible by public transportation or car. The gallery is open to visitors from Tuesday to Sunday, from 11:00 AM to 7:00 PM, with extended hours on certain days for special exhibitions and events. Admission to the gallery is free, allowing art lovers of all ages to immerse themselves in the world of modern Indian art.

Exhibition Highlights:

One of the highlights of the Jehangir Art Gallery is its rotating exhibitions, which showcase the latest trends and developments in contemporary Indian art. From solo shows by up-and-coming artists to thematic group exhibitions curated around specific themes or concepts, the gallery offers a diverse array of artistic experiences that cater to a wide range of tastes and interests.

Artist Residencies and Workshops:

In addition to its exhibition program, the Jehangir Art Gallery hosts artist residencies and workshops that provide opportunities for artists to engage with the public and share their creative process. Visitors can attend artist talks, demonstrations, and interactive sessions that offer insights into the techniques and inspirations behind the artworks on display, fostering a deeper appreciation for the artistic process.

Café and Bookstore:

After exploring the galleries, I take a moment to relax and unwind at the gallery's café, where I enjoy a cup of coffee and a light snack amidst the creative ambiance of the space. Nearby, the gallery's bookstore offers a curated selection of art books, catalogs, and souvenirs, allowing visitors to take home a piece of the Jehangir Art Gallery experience.

Chapter 9

Shopping and Souvenirs

Colaba Causeway: Shopper's Paradise

Nestled in the heart of South Mumbai, Colaba Causeway beckons with its vibrant atmosphere, eclectic shops, and bustling street markets, making it a must-visit destination for avid shoppers and curious wanderers alike. From colorful street stalls to chic boutiques and quaint antique shops, this lively thoroughfare offers a treasure trove of delights waiting to be discovered around every corner.

Exploring the Market:

As I meander through the bustling lanes of Colaba Causeway, I am immediately captivated by the kaleidoscope of sights, sounds, and smells that surround me. The market is a melting pot of cultures and influences, with vendors hawking everything from traditional Indian textiles and handicrafts to trendy fashion accessories and quirky souvenirs. With its lively ambiance and diverse offerings, Colaba Causeway promises an unforgettable shopping experience like no other.

Location and Hours:

Conveniently located near the iconic Gateway of India and other tourist attractions, Colaba Causeway is easily accessible by public transportation or car. The market operates daily, from early morning until late evening, with vendors setting up their stalls as early as sunrise and staying open well into the night to cater to both locals and tourists alike.

Shopping Highlights:

One of the highlights of Colaba Causeway is its array of street stalls and makeshift shops, where visitors can haggle for bargains and unearth hidden treasures. From traditional Indian garments like sarees and kurtas to funky jewelry, bags, and footwear, the market offers something for every taste and budget. Additionally, shoppers can browse through a selection of antique stores and art galleries, where they can find unique pieces of vintage jewelry, home decor, and artwork.

Culinary Delights:

No visit to Colaba Causeway would be complete without sampling some of the delicious street food and local delicacies on offer. From spicy chaat and savory kebabs to sweet treats like jalebi and kulfi, the market boasts a tantalizing array of culinary delights that are sure to tantalize the taste buds and leave visitors craving for more.

Tips for Shopping:

While exploring Colaba Causeway, it's important to keep a few tips in mind to make the most of your shopping experience. Bargaining is a common practice in Indian markets, so don't be afraid to negotiate with vendors to get the best price. Additionally, be sure to wear comfortable footwear and carry a bottle of water to stay hydrated while navigating the crowded lanes.

Colaba Causeway is more than just a market—it's a vibrant tapestry of culture, commerce, and community that encapsulates the spirit of Mumbai. Whether you're searching for unique souvenirs, sampling local street food, or simply soaking in the vibrant atmosphere, a visit to Colaba Causeway promises an unforgettable shopping adventure that will leave you with lasting memories and a newfound appreciation for the city's dynamic energy.

Crawford Market: A Blend of Old and New

Nestled in the heart of Mumbai's bustling Fort neighborhood, Crawford Market stands as a testament to the city's rich history and vibrant culture, offering visitors a unique blend of old-world charm and modern-day hustle and bustle. Built in the 19th century during the British colonial era, this iconic market has been a hub of activity for generations, attracting shoppers from near and far with its diverse array of goods and lively ambiance.

Exploring the Market:

As I step into Crawford Market, I am immediately struck by the vibrant sights and sounds that surround me. The market's ornate Victorian-style architecture, with its soaring arches and intricately carved facades, harkens back to a bygone era of grandeur and elegance. Yet, amidst the historic charm, the market is a hive of activity, with vendors peddling everything from fresh produce and spices to clothing, electronics, and household goods.

Location and Hours:

It is located near Mumbai's iconic Chhatrapati Shivaji Maharaj Terminus and other major landmarks, Crawford Market is easily accessible by public transportation or car. The market operates daily, from early morning until late evening, with the busiest times usually occurring in the early hours as shoppers flock to stock up on fresh fruits, vegetables, and other essentials for the day ahead.

Shopping Highlights:

Crawford Market is renowned for its diverse array of goods, catering to every need and budget. From exotic fruits and vegetables to fragrant spices and dry goods, the market is a paradise for food lovers and culinary enthusiasts. Additionally, shoppers can browse through a wide selection of clothing, accessories, and household items, with vendors offering everything from traditional Indian attire to trendy fashion finds.

Cultural Immersion:

Beyond its shopping offerings, Crawford Market offers a glimpse into the vibrant tapestry of Mumbai's cultural heritage.

The market is a melting pot of cultures and communities, with vendors from different backgrounds coming together to create a truly unique and eclectic shopping experience. Exploring the market's labyrinthine lanes, visitors can interact with locals, sample traditional snacks, and immerse themselves in the sights, sounds, and flavors of Mumbai.

Tips for Visitors:

While exploring Crawford Market, it's important to keep a few tips in mind to make the most of your visit. Be prepared for crowds, especially during peak hours, and keep a close eye on your belongings to prevent any mishaps. Bargaining is a common practice in Indian markets, so don't be afraid to negotiate with vendors to get the best price. Additionally, be sure to try some of the local street food offerings for a taste of authentic Mumbai cuisine.

Chor Bazaar: The Thieves Market

Hidden amidst the labyrinthine lanes of Mumbai's bustling Bhendi Bazaar neighborhood, Chor Bazaar, often referred to as the "Thieves Market," is a treasure trove of eclectic goods, antiques, and curiosities, where history and mystery collide to create a unique shopping experience unlike any other. Despite its notorious name, Chor Bazaar is more than just a haven for stolen goods—it's a melting pot of cultures, traditions, and stories, offering visitors a glimpse into the colorful tapestry of Mumbai's vibrant street life.

Exploring the Market:

As I navigate the narrow alleyways of Chor Bazaar, I am immediately struck by the chaotic yet captivating atmosphere that surrounds me. The market is a bustling hub of activity, with vendors peddling a dizzying array of goods, from vintage furniture and antique artifacts to electronic gadgets, clothing, and household items. The air is alive with the sounds of bargaining and haggling, creating an ambiance that is both exhilarating and intoxicating.

Location and Hours:

Located in the heart of South Mumbai, near the historic Mohammed Ali Road, Chor Bazaar is easily accessible by public transportation or car. The market operates daily, from early morning until late evening, with the busiest times usually occurring on Fridays and Sundays, when shoppers flock to the market in search of bargains and hidden treasures.

Shopping Highlights:

Chor Bazaar is renowned for its eclectic mix of goods, catering to every taste and budget. From vintage Bollywood posters and antique brassware to quirky collectibles and retro artifacts, the market offers something for everyone. Bargaining is the name of the game here, with savvy shoppers able to score great deals on unique items that can't be found anywhere else.

Cultural Immersion:

Beyond its shopping offerings, Chor Bazaar offers a fascinating glimpse into

Mumbai's diverse cultural heritage. The market is a melting pot of cultures and communities, with vendors from different backgrounds coming together to create a vibrant and eclectic atmosphere. Exploring the market's winding lanes, visitors can interact with locals, sample street food delicacies, and immerse themselves in the sights, sounds, and smells of Mumbai's bustling street life.

Tips for Visitors:

While exploring Chor Bazaar, it's important to keep a few tips in mind to make the most of your visit. Be prepared to haggle and negotiate with vendors to get the best price, but also remember to approach each transaction with respect and courtesy. Keep a close eye on your belongings to prevent any mishaps, and be open to exploring off-the-beaten-path alleys and hidden corners to uncover hidden treasures.

Local Handicrafts and Where to Find Them

Exploring Mumbai's bustling markets and vibrant neighborhoods unveils a treasure trove of local handicrafts, each piece intricately crafted and steeped in the rich cultural heritage of the region. From traditional textiles and pottery to exquisite jewelry and artwork, here's where you can find these unique treasures:

Colaba Causeway: This bustling street market in South Mumbai is renowned for its eclectic mix of stalls and shops selling a wide range of goods, including local handicrafts. Visitors can browse through colorful textiles, handcrafted jewelry, and other traditional Indian artifacts while soaking in the lively atmosphere of the market.

Crawford Market: Located in the historic Fort neighborhood, Crawford Market is a vibrant hub of activity, offering a diverse array of goods, including local handicrafts. Visitors can explore the market's labyrinthine lanes to find intricately embroidered textiles, intricately carved wooden artifacts, and other traditional Indian crafts.

Dharavi Artisans: Dharavi, one of Asia's largest slums, is also home to a thriving community of artisans and craftsmen who produce a wide range of handmade goods, including pottery, leatherwork, and textiles. Visitors can take guided tours of Dharavi to learn about the artisans' craft and purchase their products directly from the source.

Kala Ghoda Art Precinct: This cultural hub in South Mumbai is home to a number of galleries, boutiques, and craft shops showcasing the work of local artists and artisans. Visitors can explore the area's cobblestone streets to find unique handicrafts, including paintings, sculptures, and textiles, created by Mumbai's vibrant arts community.

Government Emporiums: Several government-run emporiums and craft centers in Mumbai, such as the Maharashtra State Handicrafts Corporation Emporium and the Central Cottage Industries Emporium, offer a curated selection of local handicrafts from across the state. Visitors can browse through these emporiums to find high-quality, authentic handicrafts while supporting local artisans.

Street Vendors and Artisans: Throughout Mumbai, visitors will encounter street vendors and artisans selling their wares on sidewalks and in local markets. These vendors offer a wide range of handmade goods, including textiles, jewelry, and home decor items, often at affordable prices. Exploring these local markets and interacting with the artisans is a great way to discover unique handicrafts and support the local economy.

Chapter 10

Practical Tips for the Smart Traveler

Staying Connected: SIM Cards and Wi-Fi

In today's digital age, staying connected while traveling is essential for staying in touch with loved ones, navigating unfamiliar surroundings, and accessing important information. Fortunately, Mumbai offers a variety of options for staying connected, including purchasing local SIM cards and accessing Wi-Fi hotspots throughout the city.

- **Local SIM Cards:**

Purchasing a local SIM card is one of the most convenient and cost-effective ways to stay connected while in Mumbai. SIM cards are readily available for purchase at airports, convenience stores, and mobile phone shops throughout the city. Visitors can choose from a variety of prepaid and postpaid plans offered by major telecom operators such as Airtel, Vodafone Idea, and Reliance Jio, depending on their data, talk, and text needs.

To purchase a SIM card, visitors will need to present a valid passport, visa, and proof of address, such as a hotel booking confirmation or local address. Once the necessary documentation is provided, the SIM card can be activated within a few hours, allowing visitors to start using their mobile phone immediately.

- **Wi-Fi Hotspots:**

In addition to mobile data, visitors can also access Wi-Fi hotspots throughout Mumbai to stay connected on their smartphones, tablets, and laptops. Many hotels, restaurants, cafes, shopping malls, and tourist attractions offer free Wi-Fi access to patrons, making it easy to stay connected while on the go.

Visitors can also use public Wi-Fi networks provided by the government of Maharashtra, such as Mumbai Wi-Fi, which offers free internet access at various locations across the city. To connect to these networks, visitors may need to register with their mobile phone number and receive an OTP (one-time password) for authentication.

- **Internet Cafes:**

For travelers who prefer a more traditional approach, internet cafes are available in various neighborhoods throughout Mumbai, offering computer and internet access for a nominal fee. These cafes provide a quiet and comfortable environment for visitors to check email, surf the web, and stay connected with friends and family back home.

- **Roaming Services:**

If visitors prefer to use their existing mobile phone plan from their home country, they can also activate international roaming services with their mobile carrier before traveling to Mumbai. While roaming fees may apply, this option provides the convenience of using the same phone number and plan while abroad.

Health and Safety: Hospitals and Emergency Contacts

Ensuring your health and safety while traveling is paramount, and being prepared with knowledge of local hospitals and emergency contacts can provide peace of mind during your visit to Mumbai. Here's what you need to know:

Hospitals and Medical Facilities:

Mumbai is home to numerous hospitals and medical facilities that offer a wide range of healthcare services, from routine check-ups to emergency care. Some of the top hospitals in the city include:

- **Lilavati Hospital and Research Centre**: Located in Bandra, Lilavati Hospital is a renowned multi-specialty hospital known for its state-of-the-art facilities and world-class medical care.
- **Kokilaben Dhirubhai Ambani Hospital**: Situated in Andheri West, this modern hospital offers comprehensive healthcare services, including specialty clinics and advanced diagnostic imaging.
- **Bombay Hospital and Medical Research Centre:** Established in 1950, Bombay Hospital is one of Mumbai's oldest and most prestigious hospitals, providing

quality healthcare to patients from around the world.

- **Sir H. N. Reliance Foundation Hospital:** Located in Girgaon, this hospital is equipped with cutting-edge technology and offers a wide range of medical specialties, including cardiology, oncology, and neurology.

In case of a medical emergency, dial 108 for ambulance services, which are operated by the government of Maharashtra and provide prompt transportation to the nearest hospital.

Emergency Contacts:

It's important to have access to emergency contacts in case of unforeseen circumstances. Here are some essential numbers to keep handy:

Police: For any law enforcement assistance or emergencies, dial 100 to reach the Mumbai Police Control Room.

Fire Brigade: In case of a fire emergency, dial 101 to reach the Mumbai Fire Brigade, which provides prompt response and assistance in firefighting and rescue operations.

Ambulance Services: As mentioned earlier, dial 108 for ambulance services in the event of a medical emergency. The ambulance will transport patients to the nearest hospital for medical attention.

Tourist Helpline: For assistance with tourism-related queries or emergencies, tourists can call the Government of India's 24x7 Tourist Helpline at 1800-11-1363 (toll-free) or +91-11-2250-1476.

Travel Insurance:

Before traveling to Mumbai, consider purchasing travel insurance to protect yourself against unforeseen medical expenses, trip cancellations, and other emergencies. Travel insurance policies typically provide coverage for medical treatment, emergency evacuation, and repatriation in case of serious illness or injury.

Cultural Etiquette: Dos and Don'ts

When visiting Mumbai, it's important to be mindful of cultural etiquette to show respect for the local customs and traditions. Here are some dos and don'ts to keep in mind:

Dos:

Greet with Namaste: In India, the traditional greeting is "Namaste," accompanied by a slight bow with folded hands. Use this greeting when meeting locals, especially elders or people in positions of authority.

Respect Religious Sites: When visiting temples, mosques, or other religious sites, dress modestly and remove your shoes before entering. Follow any specific customs or rituals observed at the site, such as covering your head or washing your hands before prayer.

Accept Invitations: If invited to someone's home for a meal or social gathering, accept graciously and arrive on time. Bring a small gift, such as flowers or sweets, as a token of appreciation for your hosts.

Use Right Hand for Gestures: In Indian culture, the right hand is considered clean and pure, while the left hand is associated with hygiene tasks. Use your right hand for eating, giving and receiving items, and offering gestures of respect.

Respect Elders: In Indian culture, elders are highly respected, and it's customary to address them with titles such as "Uncle" or "Auntie" (for elders not related to you). Show deference to elders in conversation and defer to their opinions and decisions.

Take Off Shoes Indoors: When entering someone's home or a place of worship, remove your shoes before stepping inside. This practice is a sign of respect and cleanliness.

Don'ts:

Public Displays of Affection: Public displays of affection, such as kissing or hugging, are not common in Indian culture and may be considered inappropriate or offensive in public spaces.

Pointing Feet: Pointing your feet towards someone or an object is considered disrespectful in Indian culture. When sitting, keep your feet flat on the ground or tucked under you to avoid inadvertently offending others.

Eat with Left Hand: Avoid using your left hand for eating or passing food, as it is considered unclean. Stick to using your right hand for all dining-related activities.

Wear Revealing Clothing: While Mumbai is a cosmopolitan city, it's respectful to dress modestly, especially when visiting religious sites or conservative neighborhoods. Avoid wearing revealing clothing or clothing with offensive slogans or images.

Ignore Customs: Be open to experiencing and participating in local customs and traditions, even if they may seem unfamiliar or different from your own. Embrace the opportunity to learn and respect the cultural diversity of Mumbai.

Disrespect Religious Beliefs: Avoid disrespecting religious beliefs or practices, even if they differ from your own. Refrain from making derogatory comments or gestures towards religious symbols or rituals.

Parting Thoughts: Leaving Mumbai with Memories

As your time in Mumbai comes to an end, it's natural to reflect on the experiences and memories you've created during your visit to this vibrant and dynamic city. Here are some parting thoughts to help you cherish your time in Mumbai and carry the spirit of the city with you as you depart:

Embrace the Chaos: Mumbai is a city of contrasts, where bustling streets and serene temples coexist harmoniously. Embrace the chaos and energy of the city, and allow yourself to get swept up in its rhythm and flow.

Treasure the Moments: Whether it's watching the sunset over Marine Drive, savoring street food at Chowpatty Beach, or exploring the hidden alleys of Colaba, treasure the moments you've shared and the memories you've made during your time in Mumbai.

Connect with Locals: Mumbai is home to a diverse and vibrant community of people from all walks of life. Take the time to connect with locals, learn their stories, and gain insights into the rich tapestry of Mumbai's cultural heritage.

Explore Beyond the Tourist Attractions: While iconic landmarks like the Gateway of India and Elephanta Caves are must-visit attractions, don't be afraid to venture off the beaten path and explore the lesser-known corners of Mumbai. You never know what hidden gems you might discover.

Reflect on Your Journey: As you prepare to leave Mumbai, take a moment to reflect on your journey and the lessons you've learned along the way. What experiences have left a lasting impact on you? What insights have you gained about yourself and the world around you?

Carry Mumbai in Your Heart: As you bid farewell to Mumbai, carry the spirit of the city with you wherever you go. Let its vibrant colors, bustling streets, and warm hospitality serve as a reminder of the beauty and diversity of the world we live in.

Conclusion

As we come to the end of this journey through the vibrant streets, bustling markets, and rich cultural tapestry of Mumbai, it's clear that this city holds a special place in the hearts of all who have had the privilege of experiencing its magic. From the majestic Gateway of India to the serene shores of Marine Drive, Mumbai has captivated us with its beauty, diversity, and boundless energy.

Throughout our exploration, we have delved into the city's rich history, sampled its tantalizing cuisines, immersed ourselves in its cultural traditions, and forged connections with its warm and welcoming people. We have marveled at the architectural wonders of Chhatrapati Shivaji Maharaj Terminus, wandered through the colorful lanes of Crawford Market, and reveled in the vibrant festivities of Ganesh Chaturthi.

But beyond its iconic landmarks and bustling streets, Mumbai is a city of stories—stories of resilience, ambition, and the unyielding spirit of its people. It's a city where dreams are born and fortunes are made, where old-world charm coexists with modern-day hustle and bustle, and where every corner holds a new adventure waiting to be discovered.

As we bid farewell to Mumbai, let us carry with us the memories and experiences we've gathered along the way. Let us cherish the moments of laughter shared with newfound friends, the flavors of exotic cuisines savored under starlit skies, and the sights and sounds of a city alive with possibility.

But let us also remember that our journey doesn't end here. Mumbai's splendor beckons us to return, to explore its hidden treasures, and to delve deeper into its vibrant culture and heritage. So, to all those who have yet to experience the wonders of Mumbai, I extend a heartfelt invitation: Come, embark on your own journey of discovery, and let Mumbai weave its magic upon you.

In the words of the great Indian poet Rabindranath Tagore, "Let your life lightly dance on the edges of Time like dew on the tip of a leaf." So, let us embrace the spirit of Mumbai and allow our lives to dance in harmony with its rhythms and melodies.

Farewell, Mumbai, until we meet again. And to all those who dare to embark on the adventure that awaits, I leave you with this simple yet profound call to action: Explore. Discover. Experience. Mumbai awaits.

Printed in Great Britain
by Amazon